CANOE PADDLES

A COMPLETE GUIDE
TO MAKING YOUR OWN

Graham Warren and David Gidmark

FIREFLY BOOKS

A FIREFLY BOOK

Published by Firefly Books Ltd. 2001

First Printing 2001

**U.S. Cataloging-in-Publication Data
(Library of Congress Standards)**

Warren, Graham.
Canoe paddles : a complete guide to making your
own / Graham Warren; David Gidmark. – 1st ed.
[160] p. : ill. ; cm.
Summary : Detailed plans and instructions on making, finishing and repairing wooden canoe paddles.
ISBN 1-55209-525-8 (pbk.)
1. Canoes and canoeing – Design and construction.
I. Gidmark, David. II. Title.
623.829 21   2001   CIP

Canadian Cataloguing in Publication Data

Warren, Graham, 1952 –
        Canoe paddles : a complete guide to making
your own

ISBN 1-55209-525-8

1. Canoes and canoeing – Equipment and supplies.
2. Woodwork – Amateurs' manuals. I. Gidmark,
David. II. Title.

VM353.W37 2001   623.8'6   C00-932616-2

Published in the United States in 2001 by
Firefly Books (U.S.) Inc.
P.O. Box 1338, Ellicott Station
Buffalo, New York 14205

Produced by
Bookmakers Press Inc.
12 Pine Street
Kingston, Ontario K7K 1W1
(613) 549-4347
tcread@sympatico.ca

Design by
Janice McLean and Robbie Cooke-Voteary

Printed and bound in Canada by
Friesens
Altona, Manitoba

Published in Canada in 2001 by
Firefly Books Ltd.
3680 Victoria Park Avenue
Willowdale, Ontario M2H 3K1

Except where stated otherwise, all photos were taken
by Graham or Susan Warren.
Back cover photo © Darel Bridges

The Publisher acknowledges the financial support of
the Government of Canada through the Book Publishing Industry Development Program for its publishing
activities.

To Sarah, Daniel, James and Susan

Acknowledgments

Graham Warren:
Thanks to the following people for their assistance in creating this book: Liz Regan, Rod Taylor, Ross Brown, Gerry Hiatt, Philip Greene, Douglas Ingram, Keith Backlund and Alexandra Conover. A special thanks to Douglas Andrews, who generously shared his immense knowledge of re-creating North American paddles.

I also want to thank my family for helping to make the paddles in this book and for their assistence in taking the photos.

David Gidmark:
For help in locating Indian paddles from various locations in North America, thanks to Douglas Andrews (Florida), Steven Augustine (New Brunswick), Jon Boucher (Washington), R. Paul Brisco (Ontario), Joe Calnan (New Jersey), Barbara Dobree (British Columbia), Wayne Doucette (Nova Scotia), Carl Pryor (Indiana), Hal Hepler (Michigan), Gerry Hiatt (Indiana), Kent Howell (New York), Carol Huntington (Vermont), Jeffery Knox (New Brunswick), Ralph Kylloe (New York), Fred McMillan (Oregon), Richard Nash (Ontario), Tom Randall (Indiana), John Rawlings (Washington), Elizabeth Regan (Massachusetts), Howard Shoemaker (Connecticut), Dr. J. Garth Taylor (Ontario), Rod Taylor (New York), Henri Vaillancourt (New Hampshire), Dr. Michael Wald (California), Mac Welles (Minnesota), Kenneth Whyte (British Columbia), Carl Williams (Connecticut), Mark Zalonis (Pennsylvania).

CONTENTS ✏

Introduction:
Make your own paddles!

With the right instruction, even the very young can learn how to make their own paddles.

Interest in paddle- and canoe-making is today perhaps at an all-time high. Canoeists are fast rediscovering the intense satisfaction to be gained by creating their own equipment rather than merely adopting the often rather soulless stuff to be found down at the canoe store.

Fashioning a paddle is a small enough project that it will not cost the earth or devour all your spare time. On the other hand, the subject is sufficiently deep that it will provide a lifetime opportunity to develop your woodworking skills, to experiment with various designs or to research the rich historical context of the craft. When you make your own paddles, you are immediately connected with the roots of canoeing, roots that stretch back hundreds, even thousands of years. Indeed, in the past, probably few canoeists did not also build their own boats as well as paddles.

Taking the time to learn paddle-making skills will ensure that you get exactly the paddle you want— a perfect fit, the blade area that you need, created with a wood that you particularly like—and all at a fraction of the price you pay for a store-bought paddle. And once you have mastered the basic skills, there are many directions you can take. You might want to progress to power tools and synthetic materials in the quest for the lightest or most efficient paddle. Or you might want to go in the opposite direction and re-create the native skills of paddle-making with an ax and crooked knife, using wood that you have harvested yourself. Why not go on to make a range of paddles to suit all moods and water conditions or build a collection of native paddles, authentically decorated, to form a beautiful and unique display?

At first glance, a professionally made paddle might seem like the kind of thing that only a master craftsperson could produce — and then only after years of practice. This is simply not the case. Even with modest woodworking skills, you should be able to get good results first time out. In a short while, you will gain a very different perspective on most commercial paddles: Why don't they balance properly? Why is the finish so poor? Why are hardwood paddles nearly always warped?

Creating something beautiful in wood evokes real satisfaction.

If you have previously practiced home woodworking limited within the confines of the straight line and right angle, you are in for a liberating experience. Although you may initially find the move away from the security of the ruler and set square a bit scary — like a first trip into the wilderness without a guide — it will ultimately become a delight. You will soon find yourself navigating through the wood freely, guided by touch and light.

Making a beautiful paddle is not that difficult. Forming its graceful curves is a technique, not an art. In fact, with quite straightforward methods, you can get your tools to cut intricate curves as surely as any basic geometrical shape. You just need to be aware of the capabilities of your tools, learn to break down the complex paddle shape into a series of simpler ones and work not haphazardly but to a system.

Anyone can make a good paddle, and *Canoe Paddles* will show you the way.

Diversity:
Evolution of the canoe paddle

A fragment of a 5,000-year-old paddle found in Denmark shows evidence of elaborate decoration. (Reproduced with permission from Acta Archaeologica)

The physics of propelling a canoe are the same the world over, so it wouldn't be unrealistic to assume that a common paddle design might therefore have evolved. A brief look at paddles from different cultures, however, quickly shows that this is far from the case, a fact which suggests that forces other than physical ones have helped to shape canoe paddles. (One exception is the paddle's overall blade area, which is conserved between quite narrow limits related to how hard a human is able to pull.)

Despite this diversity, recreational paddles have developed almost exclusively from those of the North American tradition, and this book is primarily concerned with them. It is difficult to say whether North American paddles predominate because they are the most efficient or because their shape has simply become fixed in the popular imagination, since this is the region where recreational canoeing began. It is certainly true that when asked to draw a typical canoe paddle, most people will opt for the beavertail design.

Canoe paddles are still actively evolving. Technical innovations such as double-cranked shafts and recurved blades are created under the stimulus of competition and

eventually filter down to recreational canoeists. The scientific tests on paddle blades begun by John Winters in the 1980s point the way to the future in getting paddle design onto a theoretical footing. Computer-aided design and exotic materials will undoubtedly figure even more prominently in the production of paddles in coming years. Despite this, the classic wooden paddle is always likely to occupy center stage. Wood is a supremely suitable material for paddles, being relatively light, supple and easy to work.

Much can be learned from a study of paddles from other times and other cultures. It is interesting to see how the basic concept of a paddle has been adapted to meet various local conditions and fashions, and this knowledge gives us a better appreciation of why paddles are the way they are.

PREHISTORIC PADDLES

Although wooden canoe paddles do not normally survive for long if abandoned, a significant number of fragments have been found in preserving environments such as peat bogs. The occasional un-earthing of preserved humans, or "bog people," provides the potential for one day finding a prehistoric paddle along with its owner! From wetland finds, it is becoming clear that Europe, too, has a canoe culture stretching back not hundreds of years but millennia. Amazingly, 5,000-year-old paddles have been recovered not only in recognizable form but also with still visible decoration. Some of these paddles are broadly similar to "conventional" paddles, but some are quite different, with characteristics, such as squat, heart-shaped blades, reminiscent of the South American style. It seems that European waterways were once alive with dugout craft, but they have been gone so long that they have passed even from folk memory. Why did they become extinct? Perhaps it was the pressure of population and the upsurge of technology that both required and enabled much larger planked craft to be made.

These ancient paddles often have features that tell something of the way in which they were used. One paddle, among the many found at Tybrind Vig in Denmark and dated around 3500 B.C., has a small hole at the base of the shaft which might indicate that it was tied to the gunwale in some form of oarlock. Another paddle shows evidence of repair.

Interestingly, these paddles are almost all made from ash, whereas the dugout canoes found with them are made from linden; the builders clearly appreciated the properties of the materials that they were using. The blades are finely made and generally have one cambered and one flat face, a surprisingly high-tech configuration for such ancient paddles. A small number of wonderfully decorated paddles also recovered at this site were somewhat larger than the rest, suggesting that they had a special, possibly ceremonial, role.

In the river sediment at Sainte-Anne-sur-Brivet in France, a unique discovery of more than 40 dugout canoes with associated artifacts, including paddles and 70 human skulls, was recently made.

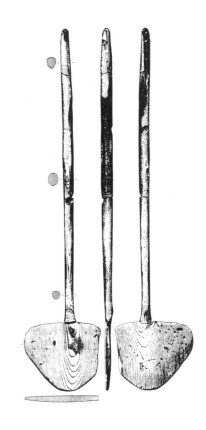

A 5,000-year-old paddle found at an archaeological site in Denmark. (Reproduced with permission from Acta Archaeologica)

An ancient paddle found entangled in roots in Two Rivers, Minnesota. The paddle is believed to be more than 200 years old and was discovered by Mac Welles. Photo by Mac Welles

By carbon dating, the canoes were found to have accumulated over a 2,000-year period, beginning around 1430 B.C. The find is particularly interesting because it shows a distinct evolution in canoe design and may do the same for the paddles once the research is complete. One theory as to why so many canoes of different ages were found in one locality is that this was a dangerous stretch of water that likely caused numerous accidents.

THE EVOLUTION OF NORTH AMERICAN PADDLES

For those who wish to pursue the history of the North American canoe paddle, the challenge of the paddlemaker's art becomes apparent: it leaves few enduring artifacts. Only a tiny part of North American paddlemaking heritage is reflected in current native tradition. Much of what is known about the origins of paddlemaking, beyond the past 200 years or so, has been gained from the relatively small number of surviving paddles, as well as drawings, often crude, by early white explorers. The great antiquity of North American paddlemaking has been inferred from archaeological finds such as slate or beaver-tooth knives, which may represent early crooked knives, the key tool of the native paddlemaker. In some rare cases, the discovery of pictographs, incised designs and even remains preserved by some freak of location have added small pieces to the almost hopelessly fragmented story of the evolution of North American canoe paddles.

Serious documentation of native canoe and paddle designs essentially began in the 1880s with Edwin Tappan Adney's research that eventually led to the publication, in 1964, of *The Bark Canoes and Skin Boats of North America*, a book which has inspired countless canoe- and paddlemakers since. Possibly the greatest single influence on historically minded boaters after the collective North American urge to canoe, it has been more or less continuously reprinted up to the present day. The book contains scale drawings of around 20 paddles attributable to North American tribes. Museums and private collections around the world contain many more paddles whose origins are less certain, or downright obscure, and can usually be only tentatively assigned to one of a number of tribes. Other valuable sources of information are the early written accounts of canoe journeys and life among native peoples. These contain many references to the use and lore of paddles.

The first white settlers in the watery regions of North America seem to have readily adopted the native canoe as the prime mode of transport. They must have adopted the paddles as well, since there doesn't seem to have been a concerted effort to convert canoes for rowing, European style. This is not to say that this never happened; an old photograph recently published shows a large birchbark canoe powered by paddles and oars, the paddlers facing forward and the rowers backward. Europeans returning home from tours of duty in North America occasionally brought paddles with them, and some of these have ended up in museums or private collections. These items would have helped to spread knowledge about what might have seemed, at the time, a rather alien form of transport. Unfortunately, the tribal origins of these paddles were not always recorded, so many of the museum items we see today are less useful than they might otherwise have been.

The fur trade voyageurs created a distinct tradition in canoe-paddle history. Their paddles evolved under different constraints, which tell their story in the shape of the blades. The lengthy journeys they undertook resulted in the adoption of narrow-bladed paddles that were less tiring to use. Wider paddles were probably used for shorter trips, and in general, there seems to have been much variation in the shape of fur trade paddles. Museum collections are a source of information about these, and occasionally, paddles, possibly of voyageur origin, turn up in swamps or sites of obvious portages or camps.

Today, paddlemaking in the native tradition is flourishing. The paddles are being made not only by native craftspeople but also by those drawn to the Indian culture. A heightened interest in native paddle designs has been stirred in those who use modern construction techniques, and manufacturers are increasingly offering "native" paddle designs in their catalogs.

It would be interesting to know how the native artisans of old, whose work we see now only in

A decorated paddle of the 1600s illustrated in Champlain's Voyages and Explorations

This Caddo design was re-created by Doug Andrews from a prehistoric engraving on a whelk shell.

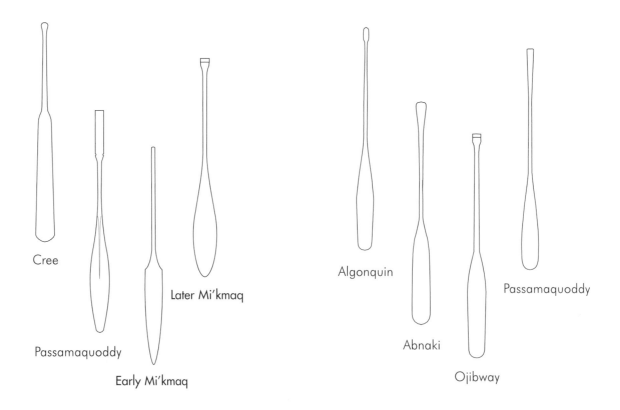

Cree

Passamaquoddy

Early Mi'kmaq

Later Mi'kmaq

Algonquin

Abnaki

Ojibway

Passamaquoddy

Above: Several Passamaquoddy-style paddles as well as an example of a Mi'kmaq paddle (far left) from the collection of Doug Andrews. Photo by Doug Andrews

museums, viewed their craft. Was making a paddle a form of artistic endeavor, or was it simply a means to an end? It is clear that if a paddle was finely decorated or intricately carved, its maker regarded it as something special.

However, even an unadorned surviving paddle can still tell us something, because the intentions of the maker leave a definite imprint on the wood. Given the chance to examine an authentic native paddle, one can learn a lot about the degree of care that went into its manufacture. Did the

paddlemaker spend time getting the paddle to balance correctly? Did the builder tolerate knots and flaws? Are the carving marks still apparent, or was extra care taken to smooth them out? One thing seems clear: paddlemaking was a very common activity. The journal of Samuel Hearne, who traveled with the Chipewyan people in the 1770s in search of the Northern Ocean, provides evidence that most members of a native group, at least in this band, were able to make their own canoes and paddles.

TRIBAL VARIATION AND ADAPTATION

There is a frustrating lack of information about the types of paddles used by North American Indians in historical times. Much research remains to be done on tribal variation, and we can only

speculate on many aspects of how their paddles were influenced by local conditions.

Paddle designs do not seem to be nearly as characteristic of specific tribes as were their canoes. In

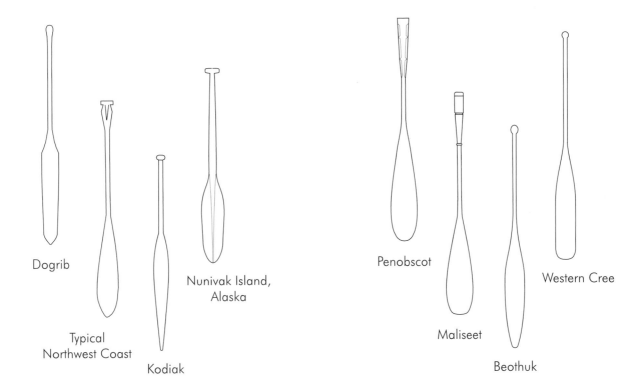

Dogrib

Typical
Northwest Coast

Kodiak

Nunivak Island,
Alaska

Penobscot

Maliseet

Beothuk

Western Cree

fact, surviving paddles attributed to the same tribe can look quite different. Given the relative ease of making a paddle compared with making a canoe and thus the greater opportunity for experimentation, this comes as no surprise. Canoe design is to some extent inhibited by its complexity—a small alteration could end up requiring adjustments throughout the structure to accommodate the change. It may be misguided to try to identify tribal characteristics too precisely. Making a paddle is basically an individual enterprise, and chances are it was (as it is now) a positive advantage to have one's paddles distinctive in case of a dispute over ownership.

Even if individual paddles varied, paddlemaking knowledge is certain to have been shared within a group and passed down from one generation to the next—knowledge such as suitable trees

to use, the best grain direction and, perhaps most important, the shaft and blade thickness required to ensure that the paddles were strong enough. It would have been essential that native paddles did not break, especially when hostile neighbors were pursuing the paddlers—their lives would have depended upon it.

Despite the fact that there was little physical reason for paddles of a band or group to conform, it is fair to assume that "fashion" would have played some role in stabilizing certain paddle design features, or decorative motifs, even if the overall blade shapes differed.

It is generally true that various paddle blade shapes differ in effectiveness in quite subtle rather than radical ways. If paddles were not pushed to their limits, then the superior characteristics of the better blade designs might not have become readily apparent. Therefore,

Top (from left to right): Miwok, Makah, Carrier, Maliseet and St. Francis Abnaki paddles from the collection of Doug Andrews. Photo by Doug Andrews. Above: Native paddles at Madeline Island Museum, Wisconsin. Photo courtesy David Gidmark

unless native canoeists took racing seriously or unless paddle design became a survival issue in escaping enemies, the pressure for paddles to evolve might have been slight. This situation would have tended to result in a wide diversity of shapes, rather than a selection for the most efficient ones.

Undoubtedly, native paddlemakers would have used the most appropriate local woods, which would have imposed certain constraints on their paddles. As an example, cedar paddles—almost ubiquitous in many regions of the Northwest Coast—need thicker shafts and blades to be as strong as the ash and maple paddles of the Eastern Woodlands. The availability of tough, durable woods might have encouraged the paddlemaker to spend more time making an elaborate paddle, whereas the effort might not have been considered worthwhile with a soft, easily damaged wood. The dimensions of obtainable trees, availability of knives and level of splitting technology could all have been factors influencing the properties (for example, blade width) of locally made paddles.

Both historic and contemporary native paddles vary greatly in the quality of the carving and intricacy of decoration. These factors clearly are related to the ability of the paddlemaker but also reflect their intended usage. Relatively crude paddles might have been quickly created as replacements for breakages while paddlers were out on a journey, whereas the finely detailed ones might have been intended for ceremonial practices or used in war.

In the case of bark canoes, later tribal styles sometimes became modified and less distinctive, owing, in part, to the increased interchange between various peoples during the fur trade. This might also have happened with paddles, although the only documented example I am aware of that may show this is the case of two Mi'kmaq paddles from different eras that are markedly different in design. Given the small number of surviving paddles, it would be extremely hard to distinguish true evolution in design from mere individual variation.

Everyday paddles

Not every paddle needs to be a work of art. Indians surrounded by rocky streams might have gone through so many paddles that they considered them disposable. Paddles made for northern rivers are frequently longer than average and heavily built with simple straight sides and flat tips. These features are required of a paddle that is used alternately to push off from rocks and to pole the canoe when the water shallows out. Sometimes the need for a canoe itself was transient and would not have justified spending a long time making fine paddles. The Iroquois made elm-bark canoes that were temporary—used briefly, then discarded. It seems likely that paddles made especially to go with such canoes would have been simply functional too.

Perhaps many, or even the majority, of the paddles ever made have not been considered worth keeping beyond the lifetime of the maker. Well-made paddles could have survived longer because they were more prized. For this reason, assessing the quality of the paddles that have survived to the present day could give a false impression of the general level of native expertise in the past. Certainly, not all surviving native paddles are well made. Indeed, some are extremely unglamorous. Travelers have commented on the sometimes crude paddles of the local Indians whom they encountered on their journeys.

One can only speculate on the proportion of native paddlemakers who were able and motivated to go beyond simple functionality when making their paddles. What is true is that the best of their paddles are truly spectacular and surpass the quality of the majority of paddles being made today.

Ceremonial paddles

Numerous documented cases depict paddles figuring in native ceremonies, rituals and rites. Certain paddles are known for which this was the primary purpose. They vary from fully functional yet extensively decorated or intricately carved paddles through to those which are so stylized as to

A ceremonial Polynesian paddle of the type used for various rituals such as protecting crops from evil spirits

be virtually useless for propelling canoes.

Champlain described a ceremony that was part of the preparation of a band of Montagnais about to set out to fight the Iroquois. The women waded out naked into the water and splashed each other using their paddles. The significance of this activity is unclear, although it sounds like fun.

Items as important to the native peoples as canoes and paddles might be expected to figure prominently in burial ceremonies. Models of a canoe and paddle found as grave goods for a Beothuk boy in 1869 are documented in Adney and Chapelle. Much of our knowledge of the transportation of this enigmatic tribe comes from this discovery.

Hunting and related paddles

Paddles have been used in the acquisition of food either indirectly — allowing the hunter to approach game silently — or directly, for spearing fish or knocking wild rice into the canoe.

"Silent running" paddles are likely to have had pointed tips and very thin edges, but apart from this, no specific blade shapes appear to be clearly characteristic of paddles used for hunting. Douglas Andrews of Florida, a fervent collector of native paddle designs, has re-created an unusual short paddle with a wraparound grip. He found that it can be used one-handed while lying in the bottom of the canoe, and he believes that the paddle's original function was for creeping up on unsuspecting ducks. This shows the value of actually trying out native paddles to

Doug Andrews displays an authentically decorated Tlingit paddle. Andrews, who lives in Florida, is an avid collector of paddle designs. He has details of some 220 paddles and has re-created well over 100 of them. Photo courtesy Doug Andrews

Some unusual paddles

A paddle with a grip that wraps around the forearm so that it can be used one-handed—it was probably used to approach prey

A paddle from Lake Titicaca in Peru that doubles as a fork for collecting tortora reed

A pair of these one-handed paddles was used by the Koryak Inuit

A paddle attributed to the Salish tribe. It has been described as a silent night-hunting paddle. The cutaway blade might lessen the chance of the paddle banging against the side of the canoe. The shape also suggests use as a weapon

A paddle design used on the Columbia River for getting a grip on the muddy bottom

Paddles as weapons

The enlarged, spiky grips on some Polynesian paddles make effective clubs—they may have had rope covers to protect the hands while paddling

The sharp point on this Nootkan paddle makes it an effective weapon

get a clue to their purpose. Samuel Hearne wrote in his journal that the Chipewyan sometimes used double-blade paddles when lying in wait for caribou at their crossing sites at rivers and narrow lakes. These paddles would have allowed the hunters to sit low in their canoes and accelerate rapidly when they targeted an animal.

Paddles with sharp points are effective for skewering fish. Many Inuit single-blade paddles show this feature, as, to a lesser degree, do many Northwest Coast paddles.

Paddles as weapons

When faced with a situation that required fight or flight, the native paddler had a most suitable implement ready to hand. In addition to providing the power for a quick getaway, a canoe paddle has considerable weapon potential at both ends.

The grip, especially if enlarged and made suitably spiky, makes a formidable club. This adaptation is seen in many Pacific paddles. The edge of the blade is also capable of inflicting considerable injury. Edges of bone were probably used to enhance the slicing action. It has also been suggested that paddles were edged or tipped with copper on occasion to increase their lethality. The cutlass shape of paddle of the Salish tribe shown in the diagram (facing page) looks like a feature designed with violence in mind. Pointed blade tips are quite common and are sometimes so exaggerated that one is left in little doubt that the paddle was intended to double as a pike. One cannot assume, however, that every paddle with a pointed blade tip was necessarily designed for fighting, be-

Carved and decorated paddles

A Maori paddle collected in 1796. The background is colored in red ocher, highlighting the pattern on the natural surface of the wood

A paddle depicted in a drawing found on the wall of a tomb in the Valley of the Kings, Egypt

A typical Northwest Coast paddle decorated with red and black pigments

cause such paddles have also been used to spear fish or to get purchase on muddy river bottoms.

Paddles for which combat was a primary rather than an incidental function were probably made to a heavier specification, resulting in some trade-off against ease of use for propelling the canoe. The extent of this trade-off presumably depended on the predisposition of the tribe for valor or discretion.

Other uses

On dry land, paddles have been used for beating cedar to liberate the fibers for clothing and ropes, as runners for hauling canoes out of the water and certainly much else besides. Peculiar notched grips have been described on some

South American paddles that might serve as props for cooking pots. Miniature paddles have traditionally been used for dances, as pot stirrers and as gifts.

Native paddle decoration

Speculation abounds regarding why native peoples in the past decorated their paddles: pure artistic expression; to establish ownership; to record events or kills; for spiritual/ceremonial reasons; as a symbol of status; or to impress their peers or suitors. Interpreting native art is a specialized subject of which I have little knowledge, but I do have one insight: surely many native people painted and carved their paddles purely for pleasure.

Detail from Voyageurs at Dawn *by Frances Anne Hopkins (1838-1919); oil on canvas; 73.7 cm x 151.1 cm; 1871. Hopkins' paintings are a unique source of information about voyageur life in the mid-1800s. This painting provides an excellent example of the types of decoration found on paddles of this era. Courtesy National Archives of Canada/ C-002773/C-134839*

Decorated Cree paddles

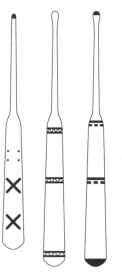

Simple designs in red pigment on Cree paddles—Adney specifically noted that the design on the left was a woman's paddle

Painting

Native paddles from many parts of the world have painted designs that range from plain coloration through simple representations of animals to intricate abstract patterns. Some designs were inscribed into the wood of the paddle, some painted on the surface. Red ocher and charcoal mixed with animal fat or fish oil were common natural pigments. The Cree are known to have used vermilion paint extensively, which they obtained in powder form by trading at Hudson's Bay Company (HBC) stores.

Certain Cree and fur trade voyageur paddles had blades brightly painted with striking colors such as vermilion or blue. This might have been to enable them to be spotted easily if they were lost overboard or left at portages. Some Cree paddles were painted green, a color more likely to be of value for camouflage. Another type of decoration often associated with the Cree is characterized by a pattern of dots, short lines and crosses, either singly or in combination. Whether this had significance beyond straightforward ornamentation of the paddle is unclear. A more elaborate abstract pattern consisting of scroll-like designs or intertwined vine leaves has been observed on Maliseet and Passamoquoddy paddles. Because of the impermanence of the pigment formulations used, it is quite possible that apparently undecorated surviving paddles might once have been painted.

Paddles with representations of familiar animals such as moose and fish are sometimes seen, motifs that might have been related to hunting activities, either for good luck or as a reminder of particu-larly memorable hunts. Northwest Coast paddles show the typically stylized art of the region in bold reds and blacks of the type that often depicts stylized totem animals and records significant family events.

Carved decoration

Paddle carving takes a number of forms, including complex relief carving of pigmented areas on Northwest Coast paddles, intricately carved leaves, simple embellishments of the structure of the paddle (such as rings or grooves encircling the shaft) and elaborate grips. It has been stated that the blades of Northwest Coast paddles intended for everyday use were not carved because that would weaken them. Carved paddles were possibly reserved for ceremonial use or were produced for sale.

This detail shows the grip of a beautifully carved Passamaquoddy paddle. Photo courtesy David Gidmark

FUR TRADE (VOYAGEUR) PADDLES

The fur trade voyageurs of the 18th and 19th centuries paddled under very different circumstances than did the native canoeists, who were largely preoccupied with hunting and fishing. The fur trade canoes needed to cover distance

(continued on page 25)

Fur trade paddle depicted in the painting *Voyageurs at Dawn*

Design taken from a replica paddle at Fort Michilimackinac

Fur trade paddle shown in a picture by Frederic Remington

A wider voyageur design—paddles of this type were probably used for paddling shorter distances

Identifying native North American single-blade paddles

In most cases, it is not possible to assign surviving historic paddles to specific Indian tribes, because their origins have not been adequately documented. Identifying a paddle is extremely difficult unless it belongs to one of the small number of tribes that made them with rather characteristic shapes.

The Northwest Coast Indians made perhaps the most distinctive of the North American paddles, characterized (naturally there are exceptions) by T-grips, thin, splayed shafts and rather pointed blades. The blade tips are pointed possibly to make the paddles effective as weapons. It has been stated that rounded paddles were used only by female paddlers, who presumably did not play a major part in fighting. Northwest Coast paddles are often spectacularly decorated with the bold artwork of this region. Red and black pigments predominate. Some distinct tribal/regional variations exist in these paddles. Cree paddles are usually of a simple straight-sided pattern with a bobble grip. Tribes of the Eastern Woodlands produced many of their paddles in the familiar beavertail shape popular today. Renowned for their slender double-blade kayak paddles, the Inuit also produced single-blade paddles. These were usually short (because kayaks sit low in the water), with a T-grip and a blade that was either a rounded oblong or very pointed.

Below are classified the design features of individual paddles that have been assigned to particular tribes with a reasonable degree of confidence. These features are not necessarily "characteristic" — that is, the classification does not imply that all the paddles belonging to the tribe had that particular design feature. This is meant to be a guide only. Identifying paddles is certainly not a science, and the best you can reasonably hope for in most cases is to link the paddle with a particular group of tribes or geographic region. Assignment is difficult, because natives were not constrained in paddlemaking by the use of a building form or template as in the case of their canoes and were probably only loosely bound by fashion and tradition. Much more research needs to go into classifying existing paddles still being produced by native craftspeople, as well as those in museums and private collections.

Detailed sketches are particularly useful when re-creating native paddles. This drawing of a Passamaquoddy paddle is by Liz Reagan

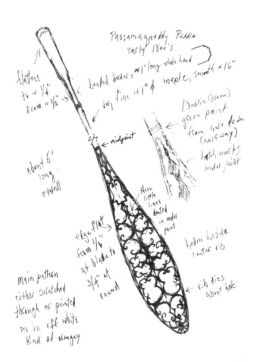

Above: The grip of paddle made by an Ojibway for a white family in 1870s. Photo courtesy Rod Taylor

Assigning paddles to North American tribes—blades

Caddo
Calusa
Timcua

Caddo-style

Iroquois
Maliseet
Passamaquoddy
Penobscot

Classic beavertail

Kutenai
Mi'kmaq

Concave shoulder, pointed

Puget Sound tribes
Salish

Dome-sided

Algonquin
Iroquois
Maliseet
Mi'kmaq
Ojibway
Passamaquoddy
Salish

Elongated beavertail

Bella Coola
Ojibway
Passamaquoddy

Ottertail

Chinook   Salish
Bella Coola   Stikine
Haida   Tlingit
Knatil
Kwakiutl
Maliseet
Nootka

Pointed beavertail

Bristol Bay Inuit   Slave
Dogrib
King Island Inuit
Kwakiutl
Lummi
Mandan
Norton Sound Inuit

Straight-sided, pointed

Abnaki   St.Francis-Abnaki
Cree   Têtes de Boule
Iroquois
Montagnais
Nascapee-Cree
Ojibway
Pomo

Straight-sided, rounded

Babine River Inuit   Pomo
Bella Coola   Salish
Beothuk   Tlingit
Chukchi Inuit   Tsimshian
Kodiak Inuit
Maliseet
Ottawa

Willow leaf

Algonquin
Cree
Dogrib
Slave

Bobble

Haida
Tlingit

Double T

Maliseet
Montagnais
Nascapee-Cree
Passamaquoddy
Têtes de Boule

Elongated, flattened

Ojibway

Elongated, flat-ended with bobble

Passamaquoddy

Elongated, "guide" style

Maliseet
Penobscot

Elongated, ornamented

Abnaki
Bella Coola
Cree
Iroquois
Pomo
St.Francis-Abnaki

Pear

Beothuk
Caddo
Cree
Kutenai
Mi'kmaq
Pomo

Pole

Kwakiutl
Mi'kmaq
Ojibway
Ottawa
Têtes de Boule

Short, flat-ended with bobble

Abnaki	Kwakiutl	Timcua
Bella Coola	Maliseet	Tsimshian
Bristol Bay Inuit	Mandan	
Chinook	Nootka	
Chukchi Inuit	Norton Sound Inuit	
Kodiak Inuit	Salish	

T

Paddles from other cultures

Certain Australian aboriginals of the Murray Valley propelled their bark canoes and dugouts in deep water with two small paddles, one in each hand. In shallower water, they used a pole that doubled as a fishing spear. It has been suggested that a certain form of spear had a removable blade and could be used with the blade as a paddle or without as a pole.

The Welsh coracle is a tiny, totally functional, totally unglamorous craft that is used to net fish in local rivers and is carried on the back of the owner. Regional variations are considerable in this traditional boat which has been in use since at least Roman times. The paddles tend to share the plainness of the coracle but do have some interesting features. Some types have blades with one cambered and one flat face; some have on the top of the shaft either a notched iron tip or a carved wooden hook to secure the paddle into the coracle during transport.

Among South American paddles is a type characterized by short, rounded or heart-shaped blades, sometimes with a point at the tip. Some are strikingly similar to the prehistoric Danish paddle already described (page 9). In fact, this shape is quite common around the world. It has been observed that in the Amazon, the pointed paddles are stuck into the mud at the sides of rivers and used for tying up the canoes; they are also used for spearing fish.

   It has also been theorized that tribes can identify approaching canoes as friend or foe by the characteristic sound that their particular shape of paddle makes in the water.

Some paddles from around the world

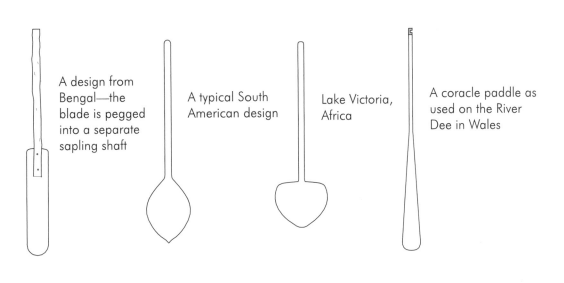

A design from Bengal—the blade is pegged into a separate sapling shaft

A typical South American design

Lake Victoria, Africa

A coracle paddle as used on the River Dee in Wales

*Location of some North American Indian tribes
(only representative locations shown—
some tribes ranged over large areas)*

Cree
Dogrib
Slave
Kutenai

Norton Sound Inuit
Bristol Bay Inuit

Kodiak Inuit

Tlingit
Stikine
Haida
Tsimshian
Bella Coola

Kwakiutl
Nootka

Salish
Lummi
Chinook
Pomo

Nascapee
Montagnais
Beothuk
Algonquin
Mi'kmaq
Maliseet
Passamaquoddy
Abnaki
Penobscot
Têtes de Boule

Ottawa
Iroquois
Ojibway

Mandan
Caddo
Calusa

(*continued from page 19*)
as fast as possible for economic reasons. The canoes were large to carry bulky loads of furs and other goods and therefore needed many paddlers to propel them. The distances covered were immense. The 2,000-mile northern trade route, or Voyageurs Highway, from Grand Portage on Lake Superior to Fort Chipewyan on Lake Athabasca, was traversed at up to 80 miles a day at 50 to 60 strokes per minute. These northern voyageurs were paddling against the clock. When the winter ice melted, they had to bring out the season's catch of furs to the rendezvous with the Montreal brigades at Lake Superior and get back before the ice re-formed. Their paddles were shaped by these challenges.

Voyageur paddles were typically very slim. Estimates vary, but blade sizes around 4 inches by 18 inches, or even smaller, are most frequently quoted. The paddles shown in the paintings of Frances Anne Hopkins, a unique source of information about the HBC voyageurs of the mid-19th century, resemble very slim otter-tails. Canoeists who have experience in paddling all day, every day, like the voyageurs did, generally find narrow paddles used at a high stroke rate to be less tiring than wider ones at a slower stroke rate.

A large Montreal canoe usually held about 10 paddlers. Together with the cargo, it was rather crowded. The paddles of the non-steering central paddlers were reputedly very short (around 4 feet), not only because the voyageurs were diminutive but also to avoid paddles clashing in the confined interior of the canoe. The bow and stern paddlers had longer paddles with larger blades that were used for steering. With so many paddlers per canoe, timing the strokes was potentially a problem, which is why the voyageurs sang songs to help synchronize their paddle strokes.

Some interesting insights into voyageur paddles have been gained from reenactments of historic canoe voyages. A team led by Jim Smithers paddled three 36-foot Montreal canoes across Canada to celebrate the 200th anniversary of Alexander Mackenzie's expeditions. Paddle breakages were common because of the arm strength built up by continuous paddling, and the team thought that the voyageurs must have made many replacement paddles as they went along. Indeed, paddlemaking was probably one of the skills required by the job. Ralph Frese's Jolliet and Marquette reenactment group broke all their spruce paddles — probably hardwood was favored by the voyageurs, especially for the large steering paddles.

Design:
The inner workings of a canoe paddle

For a means of propulsion with no moving parts, the simple, elegantly shaped canoe paddle packs a lot of complexity into a little piece of wood. To be better able to appreciate its qualities—and if necessary to modify existing designs or to experiment with new ones—you really do need to get some understanding of how a canoe paddle works and the design variables involved. The various aspects of paddle design are discussed separately here, but in a real-life situation, they work in concert, which makes things somewhat more complicated.

Neophyte paddlemakers should probably note from the outset that the perfect paddle does not exist. The best you can hope for is a very good paddle, which is a compromise between many opposing design factors—a compromise that will vary depending upon the type of canoeing you intend to do.

One overriding element is that

The anatomy of a paddle

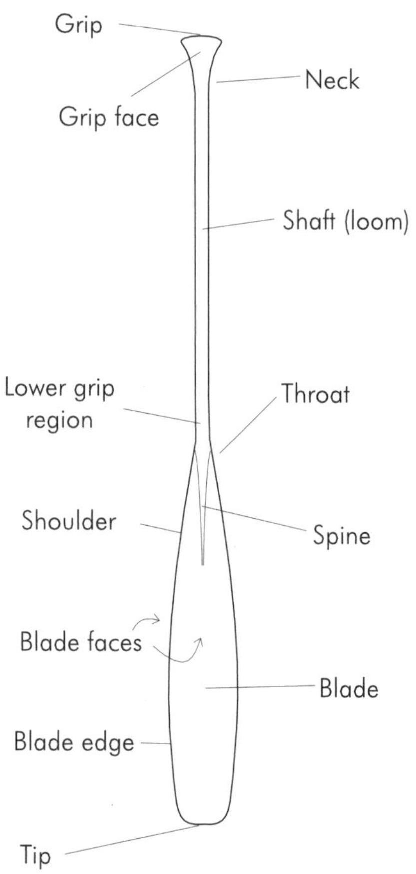

- Grip
- Neck
- Grip face
- Shaft (loom)
- Lower grip region
- Throat
- Shoulder
- Spine
- Blade faces
- Blade
- Blade edge
- Tip

Major performance characteristics

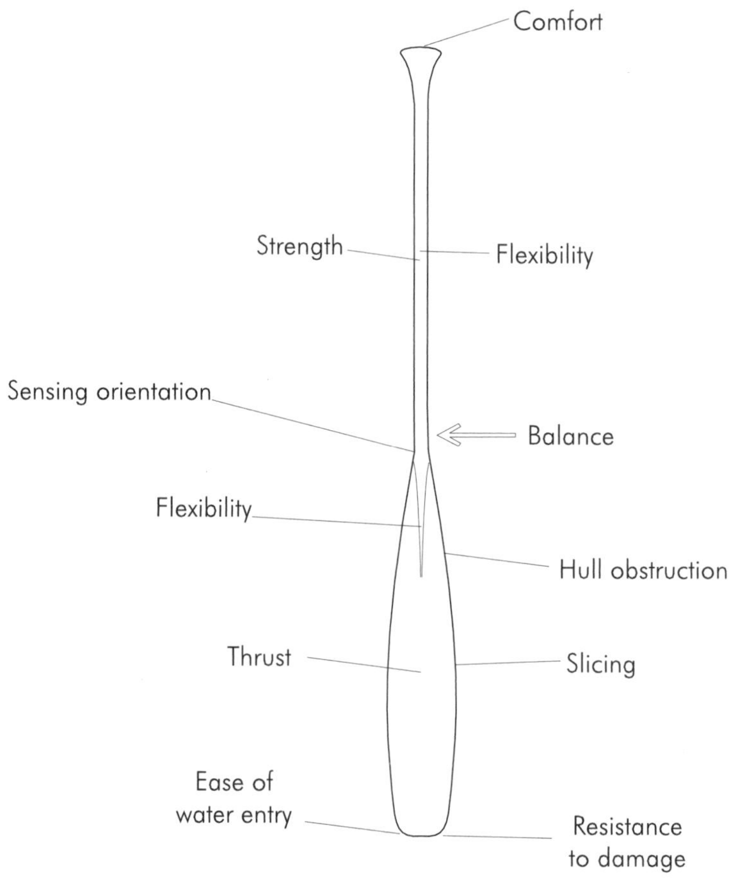

- Comfort
- Strength
- Flexibility
- Sensing orientation
- Balance
- Flexibility
- Hull obstruction
- Thrust
- Slicing
- Ease of water entry
- Resistance to damage

a paddle should have as much "drag" (resistance to movement through fluid) as possible so that it gets maximum hold on the water; another is that it should be comfortable to use, which is essentially a function of its lightness, flexibility and grip design.

Here, the various structural factors are considered in the order of the natural power train from paddler's hands down to the water below. Following that is a discussion of the intrinsic factors, such as weight and flexibility, which also affect the performance of a paddle.

GRIPS

It goes without saying that the grip should be comfortable to hold and afford a firm purchase on the paddle so that you have good control of its movements. But the significance of the grip goes beyond this; it plays a role in balancing and has a considerable effect on the visual impact of the paddle. A grip that is significantly flared is also useful for retrieving a canoe that is about to drift out of reach.

Choice of grip is subjective. To be comfortable, it must conform to the shape of your hand; if you paddle both sides, you should verify that it is comfortable in both hands. If it is too thick or too thin, you will probably have to grasp it too tightly, which will result in premature muscle fatigue. It should be significantly scooped away at the sides to relieve pressure on the inside of the thumb, which is the classic site of blisters.

I like to have a slightly asymmetrical grip, which allows me to flip the paddle periodically and get a change in shape that brings welcome relief to my hands on a long trip.

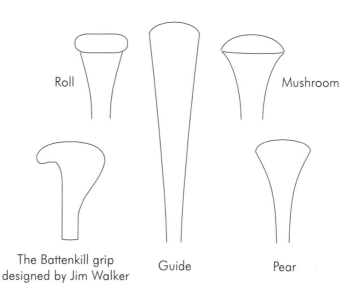

A variety of grips

Roll

Mushroom

The Battenkill grip designed by Jim Walker

Guide

Pear

People's hands vary greatly. A good way to get a personalized fit is to squeeze a piece of modeling clay and take the dimensions off this to form the basis of your grip design. The material and finish used also have a direct effect on comfort. Hard varnish is more likely to cause sore hands than is an oil finish. Even commercially made varnished paddles are frequently left unfinished (or have oil) on the top of the grip and sometimes at the lower grip region as well. Some woods are more comfortable to hold than others are. Softwoods such as pine or cedar seem to feel softer and more comfortable in the hands than many hardwoods. If you are making a laminated paddle, you can always glue in the wood of your choice for the grip.

Because of their shape, paddles tend to be naturally blade-heavy, whereas ideally, they should balance just below the lower grip region. Larger grips, such as the guide style, help to balance a pad-dle because they concentrate more weight at the top of the shaft.

Some North American native paddles, especially the earlier ones, had simple bobble grips or no grip at all. At first sight, these look extremely hard on the hands, but such paddles may have been used with both hands on the shaft, as shown in some photographs and early drawings of native paddlers. In this case, the end of the shaft was not used as a grip, and the bobble may have been present only to stop the paddle from flying out of the hands, especially during some of the more flamboyant strokes that have been described, as when the Salteaux flicked their paddles horizontally to the opposite side of the canoe between strokes. Bobble grips are actually quite comfortable when used in contemporary style; however, because they are round, you lose the ability to sense the orientation of the paddle.

Many of the cheaper modern plastic paddles have T-grips, a style that is also characteristic, although in a much more stylish form, of native Northwest Coast paddles. Although T-grips are useful for hooking the backpack out of the canoe and give a positive control of rotation of the paddle, they generally look out of place on wooden recreational paddles. Recently a hybrid half-T grip has been described. Named the Battenkill grip and seemingly designed in recognition of the fact that only one side of the hand has a thumb, it is said to be very comfortable and versatile in use.

The lower grip region of the shaft also requires a little thought. An elliptical section (perpendicular to the blade) is generally more comfortable to hold than a round one, because an ellipse is the natural shape made by the gripping hand. It also gives a tactile awareness of the orientation of the paddle. On paddles with tapered shafts, it is usual to leave the lower grip region untapered, because this is more comfortable to hold on to.

SHAFT

The primary role of the shaft is to transmit the power of the paddler down to the blade. Important secondary functions are to give ease of grip, as just described, and to dampen down shocks and so protect the canoeist's wrists and arms. The architecture of the shaft also has implications for the overall weight and balance of the paddle. The length of the shaft has to be right to establish the optimum geometry for paddle strokes, although it is possible to become accustomed to quite a wide variation of lengths by adapting your style.

The shaft has to be strong; it has to be light; it has to have a little flexibility without being floppy. These criteria are to a large extent conflicting, and resolving this three-way tug-of-war (strength vs. lightness vs. flexibility) is by no means easy. A compromise is in order. We want the strongest shaft that can be made within an acceptable weight limit that still provides adequate flexibility. A suitable compromise can be reached by a sensible combination of dimension and material. The shaft takes a fair amount of punishment against the gunwales, and so ideally, the material should have good abrasion resistance.

Cross section

In terms of strength, a round hardwood shaft of $1\frac{1}{8}$ inches (or $1\frac{1}{4}$ inches in softwood) should be strong enough for most recreational paddling, although for whitewater, it needs to be thicker. The suggested dimensions for different types of shaft are shown in the diagram. I recommend an elliptical section. It is comfortable to hold and is a little forgiving on in-

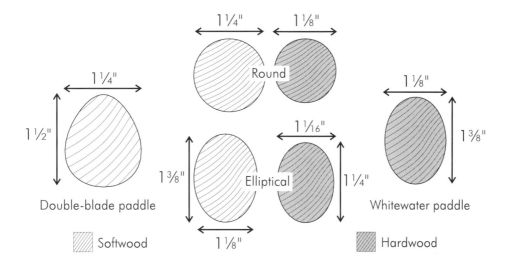

Typical shaft dimensions

Round — 1 1/4" / 1 1/8"

Double-blade paddle — 1 1/4" / 1 1/2"

Elliptical — 1 3/8" / 1 1/16" / 1 1/4" / 1 1/8"

Whitewater paddle — 1 1/8" / 1 3/8"

Softwood Hardwood

discretions by the maker—the hands and eyes can detect deviations from a perfect circle far easier than they can from a perfect ellipse. An elliptical shaft also has built-in resistance to rotation in your hands. (One advantage of a round shaft is that it is easier to use for rolling out dough when you are out on a trip.)

A more complex section is the oval. This is an asymmetrical shape, which is very comfortable to hold one way around, but not the other—a severe disadvantage for a single-blade paddle but one that is appropriate for a double.

Taper
There are advantages to tapering the shaft from the lower grip region up to the neck. I make most of my paddles with an elliptical section at the throat and taper this to a circular section at the neck. The paddle is lighter and gains a certain elegance. Maximum strength is retained lower down, where it is needed, and the shaft

develops a little more flexibility toward the grip. One disadvantage is that the paddle is more difficult to balance, because weight is removed from the grip end of the paddle, which is normally too light already. The tapering, if any, is normally in depth, not width, although you will see a few paddles that are tapered in both of these dimensions.

Length
Choosing the correct length for your paddle is a black art but is also a subject on which everyone has a definite opinion. The newcomer is likely to submerge in an excess of well-meant but conflicting advice.

In reality, it is meaningless to talk about the correct length for your paddle as a fixed quantity which can be applied to any type of paddle that you might be interested in. It is the "grip span"—the distance between the top of the grip and the bottom of the lower hand on the paddle—that is the

important fixed dimension. The length of the blade varies considerably between designs, so it is clear that when you add your fixed grip span to the variable blade length, the overall paddle length required depends on the blade design that you choose.

There is a small length of shaft below the lower hand on the paddle but above the blade, a sort of no-man's-land that people seem reluctant to talk about. For want of a better name, I call this the freeboard zone. With the grip span and blade length both fixed, this is the variable part of the paddle design where you can fine-tune the length in light of the various considerations listed later on. The freeboard zone varies from zero to 3 or 4 inches.

The easiest method for determining shaft length is to take the required length from a paddle that you are used to and have found comfortable and efficient. Add this dimension to the length of the blade that you have chosen to give

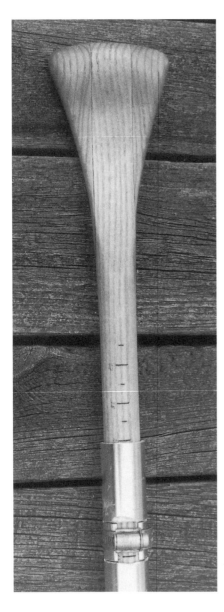

Above: This adjustable paddle can likewise be used to determine the shaft length. This model hinges at the throat to allow experimentation with degrees of bend. Top right: With the paddle-aloft method, the paddle is approximately the right size if your arms make right angles at the elbows when the paddle is held above your head. Bottom right: The length of the shaft can be varied by slackening off a hose clip that locks the sliding wooden shaft into an alloy tube. The shaft carries a scale that indicates the length.

an estimate of the overall length of the paddle that you need to make.

If you are new to canoeing or do not already have a suitable paddle, several formulas can give a good approximation of your grip span, and thus paddle length. But be aware that optimum paddle length depends on many factors in addition to your physique—the width of your canoe, its freeboard (which varies with loading and whether you are paddling single or tandem), your preference for sitting or kneeling and height of seats, among other considerations.

Formula 1: Paddler's seat to nose. Sit upright in a chair and get someone to measure the distance from the surface of the seat to the tip of your nose. This distance approximates a suitable grip span.

Formula 2: Paddle aloft. Grasp a

paddle (or a batten) in the normal way in both hands, and hold it above your head so that each arm makes a right angle at the elbow. The distance between the top of the grip and the far side of your other hand is again a rough estimate of the required grip span.

My method: Recognizing that abstract formulas don't necessarily conform all that closely to real life, I came up with a paddle with an adjustable shaft length (the "adjusti-paddle"), the idea being that a paddler should find the best length for a paddle the obvious way, by actually paddling in his/her own canoe, typically laden. The beauty of this device is that it makes it possible to try out as many different lengths as you like, paddle with them for a while and come up with a paddle that really suits you.

I recommend that at some stage of your paddlemaking career, you make yourself an adjusti-paddle. Then you can fine-tune to your optimal shaft length and gain a real appreciation of the effects of shaft length on performance. It will also make you the center of attention at canoeing events, where you will have people lining up to give it a try.

The construction of the adjustable paddle is quite straightforward and should be clear from the picture above. You need a piece of alloy tube with an inside diameter of about $1\frac{1}{8}$ inches so that a typical paddle shaft will slide freely inside it. The tube joins the blade section with a separate grip section. Two slots are cut or filed in the tube, exposing about one-quarter of the circumference of the wooden shafts inside. Two automobile hose clips are placed around the tube over these slots so that when they are tightened, they bear onto—and thus lock—the shaft sections. Adjustment is easily and quickly carried out by slackening off one of the clips with a screwdriver and sliding the shaft in or out. For a final refinement, add a scale (I used inked-in saw nicks) so that you can read off the grip span directly. Make sure your adjusti-paddle floats!

Refining the length estimate. Having arrived at a ballpark figure for the length of your shaft, you need to consider one or two more things that should help you refine the original estimate and end up with a paddle that suits your type of canoeing. These are variations in the freeboard zone of the shaft; your grip span should stay the same.

• A slightly shorter paddle is more suitable for solo, as opposed to tandem, paddling. When you are paddling solo, the canoe is likely to heel over toward your paddling side, reducing the freeboard of the canoe. The effect will be more pronounced if you like to paddle solo with your canoe intentionally heeled over. When paddling tandem, the weight of the paddlers tends to balance out and the canoe rides more or less level.

• For whitewater, you may prefer a shaft a couple of inches longer to give more leverage for steering and bracing.

• A stern paddler benefits from a paddle an inch or two longer than that of a bow paddler; it provides more leverage for steering.

Bent shafts

The bent-shaft paddle, introduced by Eugene Jensen in the 1970s, was designed to allow the blade to be

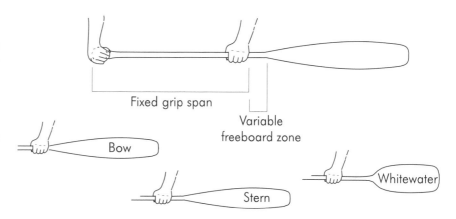

Some possible variations in the length of the freeboard zone

Fixed grip span

Variable freeboard zone

Bow

Stern

Whitewater

kept vertical throughout more of the stroke. The strokes tend to be short, and as steering is awkward with these paddles, they tend to be used in a sit-and-switch style. The shaft is bent at the throat through an angle usually in the range of 5 to 18 degrees. The angle is another compromise: a smaller angle allows some use of conventional steering strokes; a larger angle is more effective in transmitting power to the vertical blade. Paddles with around 14 degrees of bend are popular with marathon canoeists, whereas paddlers of outrigger canoes favor a 7-to-8-degree bend. The shaft on this type of paddle is typically several inches shorter than on a conventional paddle. The geometry of the com-

The name "bent-shaft paddle" is somewhat misleading. The bend actually occurs at the throat of the paddle, while the shaft is straight.

bination of blade angle and shaft length is complex, depending critically on the paddler's physique and boat. By far the best way of sorting this out is through trial and error. My adjustable paddle incorporates a joint at the throat so that the blade can be set at any angle and is invaluable for setting up the two variables in bent-shaft paddles.

A relatively recent innovation is the double bent shaft, in which there is a second bend at the top of the shaft bringing the grip more or less back in line with the blade.

BLADE

The important factors under consideration here are the blade area, blade profile (side view), cross section, aspect ratio (length divided by width), the shape (specifically the location of the widest point), the thickness of the edges and the flexibility. The blade is also, of course, the primary determining factor in the aesthetic appeal of the paddle.

Blade area

The most obvious attribute of a paddle is how much force it can apply to the water per stroke, which is directly related to the surface area of the blade. Blade areas of paddles typically range between 125 to 165 square inches. Bigger is very definitely not necessarily better, and to some extent, the choice of blade area depends on the type of canoeing intended. Very high-area blades can be useful if you need your paddle to double as a rudder when sailing. It is worth making the shaft a fraction thicker on high-area paddles to cope with the greater stresses to which they will be subjected.

Native canoeists and fur trade voyageurs almost invariably used narrow low-area paddles. This style of paddle proved to be less tiring used for long distances than the larger-area paddles popular today. Paddles with relatively small blade areas are still favored by marathon racers. Large-area blades (150 square inches and more) allow rapid acceleration and effective steering and bracing and are therefore suitable for whitewater and slalom. At the moment, virtually no manufacturer specifies the blade areas of their paddles, despite the fact that this is possibly the most important characteristic of a paddle.

Straying into the dark realm of the physics of paddling is quite an adventure. Be prepared for mysterious formulas and long words. However, the basic ideas are relatively easy to understand. A set of interacting factors comes into play when you are trying to decide on the best surface area for your paddle. These factors are encapsulated in the following relationships:

• Thrust is proportional to blade area x (stroke rate)^2.

• Sustainable stroke rate is proportional to 1/(blade area).

It is useful to break down the overall thrust of the paddle into two components: the thrust related to blade area (area thrust), and the thrust related to stroke rate (stroke-rate thrust). You can see from the first formula that stroke rate has a greater effect than blade area does because its contribution is squared. I don't know whether "thrust" is actually the appropriate physical term for what a paddle develops, but I like it and I am going to use it anyway.

A good way of visualizing these interactions is to imagine that you are using a paddle with a blade area that you can alter at will. You start paddling and slowly turn up

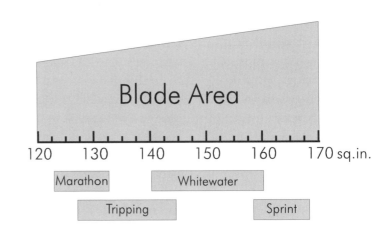

Approximate blade areas for various styles of canoeing

the blade area. As the area increases, you get more area thrust, but the energy expended in maintaining a specific stroke rate also increases, and consequently, the time that it takes you to become exhausted decreases. If, as the blade area increases, you paddle more slowly to conserve energy, you lose stroke-rate thrust. If you reduce the blade area, at some point, the area thrust you lose exceeds the stroke-rate thrust that you gain by being able to paddle faster. It is easy to imagine some "optimum" blade area at which the area thrust developed, the stroke-rate thrust and the exhaustion time achieve a balance that most suits a particular individual paddling under a given set of conditions. It would be interesting to plot out these variables on a graph. Conceptually, at the intersection of the lines sits your ideal paddle.

Of course, the real-life situation is more complex. When paddling below a certain energy output, you feel as if you could keep going all day; above a threshold value, you tire quickly. Clearly, the energy output required depends on such things as load in your canoe, wind, and so on. For tripping, the trick is to choose a relatively modest blade area that lets you operate below this energy threshold but maximizes the distance you travel. At the opposite end of the scale, in a canoe sprint race, the duration of energy output is much shorter, and you can afford to paddle fast with a large-area paddle. So there is the need to balance the blade area against the distance that you want to travel; in general, the larger the distance, the smaller the blade.

The energy output that you can sustain is obviously related to your degree of physical fitness, and I have seen physiological arguments put forward which hold that one's paddling muscles work more efficiently when operating fast than when operating slowly. In other words, you can, intrinsically, cover a greater distance paddling faster than you can paddling slower. It seems that native peoples and voyageurs, who used very slim paddles and fast stroke rates, may have unwittingly been guided by an unwritten biochemical law.

Given this rather complex scenario, how do you go about choosing an appropriate blade area? The answer is simple: trial and error. Use the recommendations given here to get close to the area that you want, then refine this out on the rivers and lakes. You should then be in possession of the information you need to come up with your "perfect" paddle.

Just to throw in an additional complication, you gain a bunch of rather mercenary benefits when you make a paddle with a small-area blade: you have less carving to do because there is less wood; the reduced weight in the blade makes the paddle not only lighter overall but also easier to balance; and because you can physically pull less water, you are less likely to damage your joints or snap the shaft.

Blade areas for tandem canoeing

When you are paddling tandem, some other considerations come into play. Ideally the strokes of the bow and stern paddlers should be synchronized to reduce the ten-dency of the canoe to zigzag. If the blade areas of the two paddles are very different, it may be difficult to keep time. Also, the thrust produced by the two paddlers should be balanced so that the stern paddler doesn't have to make excessive steering correction. If you suspect that unwanted rotation of your canoe might be because one of you is pulling harder than the other, get the stronger paddler to use a slightly smaller blade. Traditionally, stern paddlers have used paddles with slightly bigger blades to accommodate their steering role in the canoe.

Blade profile

For maximum efficiency, a blade needs to catch as much water as possible. Imagine a perfectly efficient paddle. When the paddler plants it in the water, it stays put as if set in concrete; all the force/leverage applied by the paddler is then transformed into movement of the canoe. Now imagine the real situation. When the paddler plants the paddle and pulls, some proportion of the water slides around the blade; a proportion of the paddler's energy is therefore used to push water aside and not propel the canoe. The profile (side view) and cross section of the blade are important in determining just how well it prevents water from sliding on by.

Curved-profile blades are efficient because they scoop in water and hold on to it. This is the type of profile seen on double-blade canoe and kayak paddles. Unfortunately, this profile doesn't work in simple single blades for the reasons considered later, so most canoe paddles have a straight profile.

Blade cross section

In principle, a concave cross section is best at grabbing water, but unfortunately, a simple concave section, like a curved profile, does not work at all well on a single-blade paddle. The reason is that many paddle strokes involve slicing the blade sideways in the water and/or rotating the paddle, and concave faces cause problems here. For slicing strokes, the blade must have a symmetrical cross section and thin edges, something that is incompatible with simple concave blade faces. If the blade is asymmetrical (concave on one side and convex on the other, for example, as seen in many double-blade paddles), then it acts as a hydrofoil and the blade will veer during the slicing maneuver because of the "lift" produced, resulting in loss of control. The cross section should also be symmetrical if the paddle is to be rotated, because either side of the blade must be able to act as the power face. It is only when paddles are specialized and lose the need to be used either way round (as is the case with bent-shaft and double-blade paddles) that the cross section and profile are free to be formed into a greater variety of shapes.

The next most efficient blade surface is a flat one. A symmetrical blade with flat faces has an oblong section. The problem here is that to have sufficiently thin edges to allow easy slicing, the entire blade has to be thin, which makes it weak or too flexible or both. A flat power face is usually chosen for the blade of a unidirectional bent-shaft paddle, strengthened in this case by a cambered rear face.

The least efficient surface is the cambered (convex) face, which gives a lenslike cross section. The more convex the blade, the less efficient it is, that is, the more water slides off it. This seems a little unfortunate, because it is the very shape used in most single-blade straight-shaft paddles. The reason for adopting this less-than-optimal blade face is that it represents a good compromise between drag, ease of slicing, strength and flexibility.

Another type of cross section, rarely seen on contemporary paddles but sometimes encountered on native paddles, is the dihedral face (giving a diamond cross section). This looks less elegant than the convex and is probably less efficient, but it is said to be very stable because it parts the water decisively and thus minimizes flutter (side-to-side wobble).

The usual method for making a blade thin enough to be light and to slice easily while retaining sufficient strength and stiffness is to incorporate some sort of central ridge, or spine. Spines are fre-

Various blade cross sections and profiles

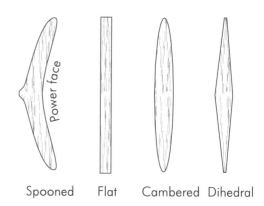

Spooned   Flat   Cambered   Dihedral

Types of blade cross section

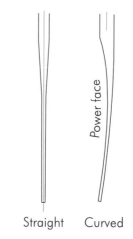

Straight   Curved

Types of blade profile

quently seen on native paddles. A spine can range from a discreet thickening merging quickly into the blade to a pronounced ridge running halfway or more down to the tip. The presence of a significant spine on the blade has been cited as a cause of fluttering.

Innovations continue to appear in the design of canoe-paddle blades, and you will hear talk of wing blades, S-blades and curved blades. In the last case, the problem of veering during submerged recovery strokes (considered to be inherent in asymmetrical blades) is claimed to have been solved by re-curving the blade edges in the opposite direction to the major curve of the blade.

Blade shape

It stands to reason that the shape of the outline of the blade (and not just its area) must affect the performance of a paddle, but apart from a couple of simple relation-ships, we are still a long way from a full understanding of this subject.

Blade shape not only influences the thrust developed by paddle but is also inextricably linked to more general characteristics of a paddle, such as resistance to tip damage, ability to shed water and degree of hull obstruction.

Noted canoe designer John Winters did some pioneering research in the 1980s on the effects of blade aspect ratio on paddle performance. He constructed a rig that pulled an approximately paddle-shaped board through a water tank under a predetermined force and timed the progress of the paddle over a set distance. The more drag a "paddle" exhibited, the slower it moved and, therefore, other things

Aspect ratio

High
aspect ratio

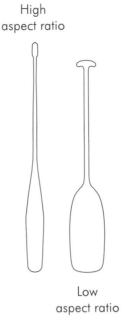

Low
aspect ratio

being equal, the more effective the shape would be as a paddle blade. He found that short and fat (low aspect ratio) blades exhibited more drag than long and narrow ones of the same surface area.

There is a need to match blade length with the depth of water, be-cause paddles should be used with the blade more or less fully sub-merged (actually, having a couple of inches out of the water is thought to be most efficient). If the blade is only partly submerged— that is, if you are using a long blade in shallow water—air gets sucked in behind (ventilation), lowering the density of the fluid at the back of the paddle and making it easier for water to slip round from the power face.

As a guide to the practical prob-lem of selecting a suitable blade shape, here are the major blade-design variables arranged in a se-ries of either/or choices, along with

some of the pros and cons of each:

High aspect ratio (long and narrow)
• Easier to keep close in to the canoe and therefore less steering correction needed.
• It is easier to carve a narrow blade than it is a wide one.
• Quieter water entry.
• Digs deeper into the water and so potentially gets a better pur-chase, because the water it reaches can be more stable, being less aer-ated and cooler (therefore denser) than the surface water.

Low aspect ratio (short and fat)
• Area for area, a more efficient shape than a high-aspect-ratio design.
• Better for shallow water be-cause of reduced risk of damaging the paddle by hitting the bottom.
• You are more likely to be able to keep the entire blade submerged in shallow water and therefore uti-lize its full surface area.
• Easier to handle: the paddle does not have to be lifted so high to get it out of the water between strokes or when switching sides of the canoe. More suitable for children.
• Makes it easier to balance the paddle, because the center of grav-ity of the blade is shifted toward the shaft.

Blade with widest point high up
• The slim tip means that the paddle has a relatively silent entry into the water.
• May be harder to keep the paddle close in to the canoe.

Blade with widest point low down
• Such a blade shape concen-trates more area farther away from the paddler's fulcrum and there-fore provides more leverage. So the paddle will be better for brac-ing and steering and may be fa-

vored by the stern paddler in a tandem canoe.

• The relatively broad tip of the paddle makes the blade less susceptible to damage, but it will probably have a noisier water entry.

Straight-line sections in blade outline

• Straight-line sections are relatively easy to mark out when making the paddle.

Outline all curves

• Some paddlers feel that straight-line sections in the blade outline (for example, the voyageur design) make the paddle less maneuverable in the water, and hence a rounded blade is possibly more suitable for freestyle paddling.

Round tip

• Slightly more stable (less tendency to flutter) and quieter in the water.

Square tip

• Slightly more impact resistance.

• Slightly better leverage (more area at the tip) and therefore higher steering efficiency. Some manufacturers used to supply paddles in pairs—a round-tipped one for the bow paddler and a square-tipped one for the stern.

Here is a final criterion: Do you actually like the shape of the paddle?

Blade shape recommendations

If paddle design is new to you, keep things simple to start with. Choose any long, narrow blade with a slim tip for deep-water tripping; a long blade with a broader tip for rougher tripping; and any short, wide blade with a flattish tip for shallow moving water. As you gain experience, you will be able to decide whether the more subtle

variations of blade design give improved performance for the type of canoeing that you want to do.

Blade surface

Theoretically, a paddle has more drag if it has a rough rather than a smooth surface on the blade. The rough surface grips the water better. John Winters made up a paddle with grit glued to the blade and believed that it pulled better, although it was not exactly a work of art. I suspect that most people would not be able to bring themselves to leave a rough surface on the paddle that they have been sweating over in the workshop; the pitying looks of their canoeing friends would be unbearable. That a canoe paddle should have a flawless, shiny surface is a way of thinking that is hard to quit. A possible disadvantage of a rough surface is that it might prevent adhering water from running off so quickly, and so the "running weight" of the paddle might be a little higher. An apparently insignificant increase could be amplified up to an appreciable weight over a paddling day.

Edges

A trade-off is also required in this area of paddle design—between ease of slicing and susceptibility to damage. Submerged recovery strokes are difficult and tiring with blunt edges. Thin edges allow the paddle to slice sideways with relative ease; the paddle acts like a precision tool rather than a plank. Unfortunately, thin edges chip easily. The safe minimum edge thickness varies with the type of wood that

you are using. With hardwoods, you can thin the edges down to about $1/16$ inch, whereas with softwoods, $1/8$ inch is about as fine as you should go.

In a laminated paddle, it is possible to run an edging strip of hardwood around a softwood core for strengthening. The edges of traditional Inuit paddles are usually strengthened in a somewhat similar way by nailing on strips of whalebone. Edge protection is especially important on such paddles, because it allows them to be used to break the crust on iced-over water to clear a way for the kayak.

Tip

The blade tip is in the front line when it comes to damage. Blades designed for use in shallow water have to exist with the increased risk of hitting a rocky bottom and so usually have broad tips. It is also usual to leave the tip of a paddle slightly thicker than the rest of the blade edge for improved impact resistance. Additional protection can be added in the form of a transverse spline, resin tip or fiberglass reinforcement.

Paddles required for reliable use in extreme environments are often tipped unglamorously with riveted-on sheet metal. Stylish alternatives can be seen on some vintage paddles from Old Town, for example, which have decoratively shaped copper tips. Inuit paddles have for centuries had shaped bone tips, which have been found at archaeological sites long after the wooden paddles themselves have rotted away.

FLEXIBILITY

A limited degree of flexibility is highly desirable in a canoe paddle. At one level, it makes canoeing more fun because the paddle feels responsive and alive. Perhaps more important, the use of very stiff paddles has been reported to increase the incidence of injuries, because shocks—when the blade hits something or when the paddler suddenly turns up the power or braces—are transmitted more or less directly to the arms. Even small shocks, the routine wear and tear of a day's touring, are amplified by the repetitive nature of the activity. In a flexible paddle, a part of this shock is absorbed by the elasticity of the blade and shaft. I have heard of canoeists getting almost instant relief from sore arms when changing to a more flexible paddle.

As with several other aspects of paddle design, there are marked differences of opinion about paddle flexibility. How much flexibility is optimum? What is the best flexibility profile? If a paddle is too bendy, then an appreciable amount of energy will be used to bend the wood rather than to drive the canoe forward. Some but not all of this energy might be regained by the flip of the blade at the end of the stroke as the paddle straightens.

Some canoeists prefer a rather flexible blade and a stiffer shaft; others opt for a more or less uniform bend along the paddle. I am one of the latter. Whatever you choose, I suspect that it is important to have a smooth gradation of flexibility from blade to shaft, be-

cause an abrupt change in flexibility here would concentrate the stresses of paddling and create a weak point at the throat.

It is easy to estimate the flexibility profile by bracing a paddle against the floor at an angle. You will need to try this out on a number of paddles to get a feel for the differences. It will take a while to relate this to how the paddles feel in use, but you should end up quite quickly with a good idea of how you want your paddles to flex.

To measure the overall flexibility more precisely, place the paddle horizontally with a support at each end and hang a weight from the middle. I support paddles across two benches 4½ feet apart and hang 22 pounds of gym weights from the center. A displacement of ¾ to 1 inch at the middle, with a uniform bend, is about right. If you want to get more technical about it, you can measure the displacement from the horizontal at several places and get a better idea of the flexibility in the various regions of the paddle. If you set a paddle that is weighted in this way oscillating up and down, the time taken for the oscillations to die out is a measure of the damping effect of the paddle, a possibly significant but virtually unexplored aspect of paddle design.

The main control you have over flexibility when making a paddle is via the dimensions of the blade and shaft. It is a simple matter to thin down a blade to make it a little more flexible. The shaft dimensions recommended in this book should produce a paddle that has a reasonable degree of flexibility, but you may want to modify these dimensions to accommodate a particular piece of wood that is stiffer or more flexible than usual or to customize the flexibility to your own requirements. The best time to assess the flexibility of the shaft is while you still have it in oblong section, because it is then easy to reduce the size uniformly. It follows, then, that you should start with the blank shaft thicker than you are likely to need so that you can work down to the flexibility you want. If you encounter the opposite situation and find that the blank shaft is too flexible, it is a relatively easy matter to glue a thin strip top and bottom to stiffen it up. But be aware that a seemingly small increase in the dimension of the shaft has a big effect on flexibility.

Slimming down a shaft once it has been rounded is more difficult because of the need to keep a fair cross section. Techniques exist for uniformly thinning a rounded shaft but are beyond the scope of this book.

Specific types of wood can be chosen to influence the final flexibility of the paddle, although this has less effect than the dimensions of the cross section. Sassafras is especially noted for its flexibility; cherry is also quite limber; ash and maple are noticeably stiffer. Different pieces of the same wood can be markedly different in their willingness to flex, and so you need to judge them individually. With laminated paddles, you have the luxury of being able to test the flex in the shaft and modify, if necessary, before you start to make the paddle.

A more subtle type of flexibility is torsional flexibility. If you hold a paddle vertically, blade immobilized between your feet, and twist the grip, you will feel a certain resistance to rotation. More resistance to rotation is better than less, because excessive torsional flexibility will dissipate some of the energy that you thought you were applying to the water. The dimensions given in this book should produce paddles with adequate stiffness, but if you find that your paddle does twist more than you would like, add $1/16$ inch to the width of the shaft on your next one.

WEIGHT

A paddle should be as light as possible while retaining sufficient strength and rigidity. A paddle weighing in at 2 pounds is typical for a standard one-piece construction, although paddles can be made a lot lighter. The main areas where you can save weight are in the slimness of the blade and by incorporating lighter woods. Extremely light paddles are made by using ultralight but fragile woods encased in fiberglass or carbon fiber.

However, weight cannot be removed indiscriminately to lighten a paddle, because the overall balance between the shaft and blade should be maintained. Slightly heavier paddles are reported to be more stable (less easily deflected by the current) in wild water.

Everyone knows that a small difference in the weight of a paddle makes a very large difference in the amount of weight you have to lift during a day's paddling; small differences are amplified out of all recognition by the 20,000 paddle strokes that this might involve.

When you really think about it, the simple concept of weight of a canoe paddle turns out not to be quite so simple after all. When you lift a paddle between strokes, what you are actually lifting is the paddle plus the film of adhering water, which can constitute a considerable extra weight. Important factors that govern the amount of water retained on blade are the surface area and the speed at which water runs off, which is related to its shape. Actually, water doesn't just run off; it gets thrown off by centrifugal force and momentum. Just watch next time you are paddling. This ejection of water is related to the type of stroke and feathering angle. The type of finish (oil or varnish) on the blade may also affect water adherence. This is uncharted territory, and my own experiments are ongoing but as yet incomplete.

BALANCE

The balance point of your paddle is a factor that perhaps you will not be overly concerned with during your first few paddlemaking projects, but it is one that will be increasingly on your mind as your skill increases. An ill-balanced paddle works, but a balanced paddle works a whole lot better.

A paddle that is well balanced is a delight to use. It seems to hover in your hand rather than be just dead weight. The ideal is to have the paddle just blade-heavy when supported at the bottom of the lower grip region so that the blade naturally presents itself to the water. As with the case of overall weight, the question of balance is a little more complicated than at first sight, because you need to allow for the weight of the adhering water film. In practice, this means that the dry paddle should be slightly blade-light, that is, it should dip toward the grip when balanced on your finger.

Another point to remember is that the finish (oil or varnish) on the paddle will affect the balance point because of the larger surface area of the blade compared with the shaft. A paddle balances when the volume of wood on either side of center is the same, but the surface area on either side of the balance point may be quite different. Four coats of varnish can increase the weight of the blade relative to the shaft considerably.

Most paddle designs tend to result in the blade being too heavy. Although you can thin down the blade until the paddle balances, you have to be careful doing this,

because it may result in the blade being too flexible or prone to breakage. Another option, available if you make a laminated paddle, is to incorporate strips of a light wood such as basswood into the blade. It is a matter of trial and error to find the width of strips needed to balance a specific paddle design, and it has to be done individually for each paddle that you make, because the balance point clearly depends on the shaft length. A third factor in balancing a paddle is the grip. Large grips, such as the guide design, are useful for balancing large-area blades.

Whenever you make a paddle to a new design, it is something of an experiment in terms of balance. You really have to make the paddle to be able to find out what you need to do next time to get it to balance properly. If the prototype turns out to be blade-heavy, then the best course of action is to incorporate a bulkier grip. Another option that is sometimes used is to add weights, in plugged holes, to the grip.

When dry, a paddle should balance a couple of inches up from the throat, above. In use, a water film adds to the weight of the blade, and the paddle should then balance at the throat.

Woods and Adhesives:
A guide to choosing your materials

A selection of paddle woods, from left to right: spalted beech, which makes very decorative laminated grips, ash, maple, cherry and mahogany.

At some time or another, most woods have probably been used to make canoe paddles. Native paddlemakers surely would have selected the most suitable local woods where possible but might have been forced to use less desirable species in emergencies or when traveling in regions where good trees were scarce. Different woods are favored depending largely on the geographical distribution of species. For example, maple is commonly used in the Eastern Woodlands of North America, whereas yellow cedar is used extensively along the Northwest Coast.

Few of us are lucky enough to be able to go out into the woods and select our material at the ultimate source—the standing tree. For those who are, David Gidmark gives advice in Chapter 10. For the rest of us, it is usually better to buy ready-sawn timber at a sawmill than at a do-it-yourself store, because the wood is cheaper, there is more choice, and sawyers often turn out to be rather interesting people who can teach us much about wood.

Regardless of species, the most important thing to look for when choosing wood for a paddle is straight grain. Kinks or swirls in the run of the grain indicate weak areas in which stresses are localized rather than evenly distributed when the wood is flexed. Such wood is also much harder to carve. Look for imperfections on both sides of the boards and also along the edges. Reject boards from the butt end of the tree, where the grain tends to curve outwards. Most of the wood that I use has roughly 15 to 20 grain lines per inch. Knots are best avoided, although they can be tolerated if they end up in the less critical blade and grip regions of the paddle, where they can sometimes be used to artistic effect. Never allow knots or kinks in the grain to be used in the shaft. Even straight-grain wood should be used carefully in the shaft, because this is so obviously crucial to the strength of the paddle. Grain should be "contained," that is, it should run parallel to the long axis of the shaft, for if it crosses the shaft at an angle (grain "breakout"), the paddle will be much weaker.

GRAIN DIRECTION

For a one-piece paddle, it is most usual to select wood that is flat (plain) sawn so that the grain laminations end up stacked front to back in the finished paddle—the orientation that creates a blade least likely to split. However, quarter-sawn (edge grain) timber is also perfectly suitable, and for most

paddling, the difference in strength is unlikely to be significant. Quarter-sawn timber is often much easier to carve and more stable during changes in moisture content, therefore less prone to warping, which is a consideration for wider blades. Unless the timber is from a really large tree, flat-sawn planks have a distinct curve to the grain that could result in warping.

Differences in the flexibility of a wood can depend on the grain direction. I once became enthusiastic about exploring this variable and made a jig for measuring the deflection of a piece while I hung a series of weights on it. I found that

Grain direction in the shaft is important

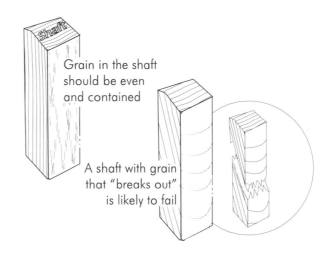

Grain in the shaft should be even and contained

A shaft with grain that "breaks out" is likely to fail

the flexibility of a piece of wood of the dimensions of a paddle shaft was very similar whether it was bent with or across the grain.

At the end of the day, both grain orientations make good paddles. Flat grain is most suitable for whitewater because of the reduced risk of splitting, but quarter-sawn is equally good for everything else. If you can't decide which to use, it is always possible to combine the various properties by laminating strips with different grain orientations.

On account of the scarcity of good wood in the United Kingdom, where I live, I have made many paddles with grain angled across the paddle and not encountered any problems either with warping or splitting. I prefer to use angle-grain stock in laminated paddles, with the grain direction reversed on either side of center.

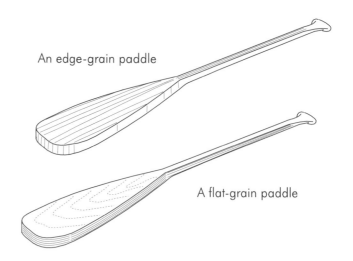

Grain orientations

An edge-grain paddle

A flat-grain paddle

CHOICE OF SPECIES

Although you can, to some extent, choose a wood to suit the intended use of the paddle, the major factor influencing the choice may well be availability. The following list gives properties of the more common woods and indicates particular applications where appropriate.

This information relates specifically to seasoned wood used for paddlemaking with contemporary tools. In Chapter 10, David Gidmark imparts extra advice about selecting woods for making paddles using an ax and crooked knife.

The properties of various woods can be blended in a laminated paddle so that you can make, for example, a tough but relatively light paddle by having something like basswood (light) for the inner lam-

inations and ash (tough) for the outer ones. Strength and lightness are opposing characteristics, and some kind of compromise has to be reached, depending on the type of canoeing that you plan to do. A tough, hard and therefore weighty wood is a sensible choice for maneuvering a heavily laden canoe out on a trip or for whitewater canoeing, whereas a light paddle can be a joy to use for a short skim on the lake in a light boat. A softwood shaft is more prone to damage by chafing against the gunwale than is a hardwood one.

Ash
Weight: heavy; 43 lb./cu.ft.
Abrasion resistance: high
Ash is perhaps the best all-

round wood for paddlemaking and is the wood of choice for rugged tripping paddles. To work with it, you will need sharp tools, but even so, the grain tends to pull easily if you plane it in the wrong direction. This makes carving laminated ash paddles—where the grain might run in several different directions—quite a frustrating experience for the beginner.

Several species of ash are harvested commercially, but their properties are quite similar. The wood can have a very attractive figure (pattern of growth rings) but has an open grain that makes it difficult to get an ultra-smooth finish. You will be able to find pieces of ash in a number of shades, ranging from almost white to a chocolaty brown. Combining these shades by laminating can result in subtly beautiful paddles. Another consequence of the open grain is that in laminated paddles, glue gets squeezed into the texture of the wood, making the glue lines look ragged (although this is a problem only with dark glues).

Probably the strongest wood available is "sports-grade" ash (used for hockey sticks), which comes from rapidly growing trees—6 to 10 rings per inch—harvested before they are 80 years old.

Take care when sanding ash, because the dust is carcinogenic.

Basswood

Weight: light; 26 lb./cu.ft.
Abrasion resistance: low

Basswood has some very good and some very bad characteristics. It is a truly easy wood to carve and, hence, a favorite for decoy carvers. It is also quite light, reasonably strong and inexpensive, at least in the United States. This is the good news. Basswood reveals the wayward side of its character, though, when it comes near water. It moves quite appreciably in response to changes in moisture content and consequently warps easily. As a result, basswood is perhaps best used stabilized by other woods in a laminated paddle. It is also porous and so sucks up water, especially from the exposed end grain at the tip of the paddle if the protective coating (varnish or oil) is damaged. Water creeps under varnish and will quickly lift off the finish. It follows that basswood must be kept well sealed.

Basswood makes light but high-maintenance paddles.

Birch

Weight: heavy; 41 lb./cu.ft.
Abrasion resistance: high

Birch is a good wood for paddles, because it is strong and relatively easy to carve.

Cedars

Weight: light; 22-25 lb./cu.ft.
Abrasion resistance: low

Properties vary markedly among the many different types of cedar. White cedar is better than western red, because it is not as brittle.

One-piece paddles that are to be used carefully in deep water can be made with cedar. Cedars are also a fine choice for feature strips in a blade, provided the tip is strongly splined crossways to reduce the risk of splitting. These woods are especially useful for paddles that are to be sheathed in fiberglass—you can then take full advantage of their good looks and light weight but not be at the mercy of their weakness.

Cedar dust is carcinogenic.

Cherry

Weight: medium; 38 lb./cu.ft.
Abrasion resistance: medium

Cherry is an attractive, mid-toned wood. It is relatively easy to carve and very easy to sand. It is strong enough for one-piece "Sunday best" paddles that are going to be well looked after.

Douglas Fir

Weight: medium; 32 lb./cu.ft.
Abrasion resistance: medium

This wood is readily available in clear lengths. Pieces with a low number of growth rings (fewer than 10 lines per inch) have grain that pulls rather easily under the plane. Douglas fir has a reputa-

It is easier to cut large pieces of wood with a hand-held circular saw than to maneuver the wood on a saw table. Note the small wedge used to push into the saw cut to prevent the wood from closing up on the blade. Watch out for end checks, as can be seen in this slab of cherry.

Pine

Weight: medium; 30 lb./cu.ft.
Abrasion resistance: low

The general name "pine" covers several species of pine and fir, and their properties vary quite widely. Oregon and Columbian pine have been reported to splinter rather easily. The wood is readily workable because it is relatively soft and the grain cuts predictably, and so it is an excellent choice for the novice paddlemaker. Wood with a high resin content has the nasty habit of clogging sandpaper quickly.

Spruce

Weight: light; 24-27 lb./cu.ft.
Abrasion resistance: low

Sitka spruce is by far the best of the several different types of spruce available. A spruce paddle is light and springy; the wood represents a good compromise between strength and lightness. It is a recommended wood for light-use paddles.

The density figures quoted here are average values. Within a species, the density can vary from tree to tree, depending on differences in genetic constitution and growth conditions; it can even vary between different parts of the same tree. Select the lighter ones, which are generally preferable, by lifting several pieces.

Bear in mind that you will be paying for the wood by total volume, not by the amount of usable material; so, unless you can use the lower-grade off-cuts for other projects, you may want to reject boards that contain good regions but an unacceptable amount of waste.

You are at a distinct advantage if you have the tools available to allow you to resaw your stock tim-

tion for splitting rather easily, and so it is probably best used as strips in laminated paddles, where it introduces an unusual tan color. It is best avoided in whitewater paddles unless they are to be fiberglassed.

Mahogany

Weight: medium/variable
Abrasion resistance: medium

The many species of mahogany are generally rather weak wood best used for dark feature strips.

Maple

Weight: heavy; 45 lb./cu.ft.
Abrasion resistance: high

Maple makes very good one-piece paddles and is also useful for exterior strips on laminated blades incorporating softer woods. It is quite easy to carve with sharp tools and sands to a smooth finish. If not kept well sealed against moisture, it has a slight tendency to split at the blade tip. A good choice for working paddles.

ber into usable pieces. Quite apart from saving the cost of having the supplier cut the wood for you, which can be considerable, resawing at home will give you time to think about the best way to divide up the pieces. This task is difficult to do amid the deafening confusion and seemingly life-threatening conditions in the sawmill, with the cost of the sawyer's time mounting all the while, but it is quite easy in the relative tranquility of your own workshop. As you gain experience, you will be able to utilize your wood more economically, using the "waste" between one-piece paddles for the shafts, blades or grips of laminated paddles, giving full consideration to the grain direction and position of imperfections such as small knots or kinks in the grain.

Another benefit of resawing is that by observing what happens when you cut into it, you get useful clues about the stresses that are locked within your plank. If the cut stays a uniform width and the piece simply falls in half, then you have yourself a good, relaxed board. If the cut is releasing pent-up stresses in the wood, the ends emerging from the blade may splay apart, arch up or down or bend inwards and trap the blade. Have a couple of slim wedges handy that you can insert into the cut if it does show signs of closing up. Stresses can build up in the structure of the wood if drying is uneven or if the original tree itself was twisted or grew on a slope. The stresses in kiln-dried wood are likely to be greater than in material that is air-dried, because in the latter, the fibers have more time to relax. To a large extent, the quality

of kiln-dried wood depends on the drying regime used. Use air-dried timber if you have the choice. Wood that has bowed during resawing should be hung for at least a couple of weeks to let the twists come out fully, following which the timber can be trued up. Slightly bent strips can be used in laminated paddles directly by gluing up so that the bends in the individual pieces are opposing and thus cancel each other out.

You must also be aware that resawing is a dangerous activity. Take the time to learn a safe system of operation and *never* deviate from this, even if at times it seems overly determined. Having the system ingrained into your subconscious could be the only thing standing between you and disaster if you are distracted when sawing—a common cause of accidents. You must also take precautions against exposure to toxic wood dust by wearing a suitable mask and preferably using a dust extractor as well.

Large, heavy pieces of timber are quite difficult to resaw. Use a bandsaw, if possible. If you have to use a circular saw, it is usually better with very large pieces to use the saw hand-held, guided with a fence, if the starting piece happens to be straight, or by a batten securely clamped down. It is easier to move the saw than it is the wood. To reduce the risk of the blade jamming and causing the saw to kick back, you must use a saw fitted with a riving knife. Even when you take this precaution, however, there is a high risk when cutting thick pieces (3 inches or thicker) of hardwood if the cut releases stresses and the wood turns in and traps the blade. I know this from experience. Not only did I have an extremely ugly, out-of-control piece of machinery in my hands, but the episode also wrecked my $400 saw. If at all possible, have the basic cuts on thick stock done at the sawmill.

Adopt a routine when you bring new stock home. If it is newly cut wood, mark on the date so that you will know when it is fully seasoned. Look each board over closely on both sides, and mark boldly with a felt-tip pen the position of splits, knots and other imperfections. This will help you avoid using a piece of flawed timber inadvertently. Look the board over once again to double-check. Examine for wormholes, and treat these with wood preserver; you do not want to start an epidemic in your store of wood. It is good practice to go through all your stock periodically and check for new insect damage. Finally, store

your timber correctly. The best way to do this is to stack it horizontally with thin battens between the individual pieces to allow airflow. Leaning pieces against a wall for prolonged periods may induce bending.

Certain pieces of wood are particularly suited for specific uses: a narrow piece with very straight grain may be especially good for the shafts of laminated paddles, and short lengths are good for blade laminations. I like to write this on the piece right away, before it goes on the stack.

You might like to keep a lookout for small pieces of unusual woods, such as yew or spalted material, which can be used to good effect for the grips of laminated paddles. Once word gets around that you collect wood, you may well be inundated with offers of small but usable pieces of timber at tree-pruning time. Paint the ends to

prevent rapid water loss, and allow the wood to season slowly outside, under cover, rather than in a heated workshop. Rapid drying almost invariably causes cracking. *The Woodworker's Bible* provides excellent advice on seasoning wood.

Reclaimed wood is often a good source of material for paddles and can be of excellent quality if it belongs to an era when good wood was less scarce than it is today. But I am always a bit on edge when using reclaimed wood because of the ever-present risk of hitting a well-camouflaged nail, which could do possibly costly and certainly annoying damage to tools.

Always buy timber that is at least 6 inches longer—even longer is better—than the paddle that you want to make. This gives you a safety margin for discarding the ends of the board, which usually harbor drying-out cracks (end checks).

ADHESIVES

Choosing the glue for making laminated paddles is a little more complicated than you might think. The ideal adhesive would be one that is strong, totally waterproof, able to cope with the swelling and shrinking of wood in relation to moisture, of long shelf life, transparent and kind to your tools. I have not yet found such a glue.

Strength and resistance to water are easy to come by; many glues possess these qualities. In contrast, few types of glue also have the flexibility necessary to move with wood as it expands and shrinks (so-called hydrocycling). The demands on a glue are more severe in this respect if the strips glued

together are of different woods that have markedly different responses to moisture. Clearly, the extent to which a wood changes shape in relation to moisture content will depend upon how much water enters the paddle, which in turn effectively depends on how well the sealing finish on the paddle is maintained. Most moisture enters at the edge grain at the blade tip.

If using an old stock of glue of unknown expiry date, it is wise to do a setting test. Delayed setting is usually the first sign of trouble. Make up the glue in exactly the proportions specified by the manufacturer, and note the setting time,

taking account of the temperature. If the setting time is appreciably longer than what the maker claims, do not use the glue.

Most glues are quite toxic, so you must wear rubber gloves and also a dust mask when handling the powdered components. Eye protection is also sensible. Work in a well-ventilated area.

Urea-formaldehyde (Cascamite, Aerolite)
This type of glue comes as a convenient powder (with a long shelf life) that you simply mix with water. It is relatively strong but water-resistant rather than totally waterproof, and it appears to toler-

ate hydrocycling. It dries to a transparent glue line. I have used this glue quite extensively for touring paddles and have never had one fail. Regarding its water-resisting qualities, I did a test in my pond with strips laminated from different woods glued together with Cascamite, and even when the wood began to rot, the glue still showed no signs of letting go.

Resorcinol-formaldehyde (Cascophen, Penacolite)

This adhesive is claimed to be totally waterproof, extremely strong and resistant to hydrocycling. It is reputed to be the only glue approved for use in marine plywood because of its resistance to boiling. Sounds good, but there are disadvantages. Firstly, it has a shelf life of only one year. This means that many stores will not stock it, and by mail order, it is frequently available only in large sizes—far more than the average woodworker can use in one year.

The second problem is that the glue is a dark brown that gives a ragged glue line where it becomes squeezed into an open-grain wood such as ash. This is not a problem with smooth woods like maple, but even so, it still highlights any places where glue joints are not as narrow as they should be. Conversely, dark glue lines can look rather striking with some woods and so add to the beauty of the paddle.

A third problem is that this glue is quite fussy with regard to setting temperature and should be avoided if your workshop is likely to fall below around 50 degrees F.

A particular vice of this glue is that it stains kitchen sinks and

work surfaces. This even applies to quite dilute washings, so I recommend cleaning rubber gloves, glue pots and the like outside.

Epoxy (West System 105/206)

Epoxy is very strong and transparent, has reasonable shelf life and is very convenient to use, especially if you invest in a pair of pump dispensers that give you the resin and hardener in the correct ratio. Unfortunately, epoxy is rather notorious for being intolerant of hydrocycling. It also dries extremely hard and blunts tools quickly. Despite these problems, it is used quite extensively by paddlemakers. The potential hydrocycling problems can be minimized by laminating strips of woods that respond in a similar way to moisture and by keeping the paddle well sealed so that water doesn't have much chance to get in. The blunting property of the glue can be circumvented by machining the wood after the glue has set but before it has fully cured—about 18 hours after gluing is about right here in the cool United Kingdom. The glue will cure faster in hotter climates.

There is now a range of modified epoxies that are claimed to have improved characteristics, including better flexibility, but I have no firsthand knowledge of these.

Polyurethane (Excel, Titebond, Gorilla)

Paddlemakers who have tried the newer polyurethane glues speak highly of them. They are reputed to be waterproof and less hard than epoxy, so they flex a little and are kinder to tools.

Native glues

Native Americans used glues based on moosehide and bison's eyeballs, among other things. I have little information on the suitability of these for paddlemaking. Locating a source could be difficult.

Overall recommendation

For a varnished, well-maintained paddle or an oiled paddle made up of strips of wood of similar expansion response to water (see Chapter 8), any of the above adhesives are suitable. I find epoxy the most convenient to use. For oiled paddles made from dissimilar woods, I strongly recommend a resorcinol glue.

Tools:
Select your level of technology

If you appreciate wood, chances are you will also be interested in tools. For most people who work with wood, this interest borders on passion. Good tools are hard to resist. The way in which manufacturers now display tools in their catalogs, with the light glinting off the polished steel blades, almost constitutes an unfair sales tactic.

You can make a canoe paddle with very simple or very complex tools. Traditionally, paddles were made with an ax, a crooked knife and a piece of glass or slate to scrape the surface of the wood to a smooth finish. This tradition survives, but the list of tools below shows how far the average paddlemaker of today has strayed from these bare essentials. Different people want different things from paddlemaking—from the complete involvement of using an ax and crooked knife through to the creative challenge of dreaming up jigs and templates to allow the production of this complex shape with power tools. But even if you start out just wanting a canoe paddle in the minimum time with the minimum effort, it is quite likely that you will become caught up in the process and be moved to slow down and experience the greater level of active participation that simple hand tools bring. You might well find yourself "progressing" backwards down the technology spectrum.

Whatever level of technology you decide to use, don't buy cheap tools. It is far better to get a good brand secondhand than a poor one new.

You will find it a whole lot easier to make a good paddle if first you get into the right frame of mind. Successful paddlemaking requires considerable attention to detail. A fine way to start building this mental attitude is by tuning into the characteristics of the tools that you need to gather together.

TOOLS FOR MARKING OUT

Pencils
Even choosing a humble pencil deserves some thought. Hexagonal pencils stay put, whereas round ones roll away; wood-colored pencils get lost, but brightly colored ones stand out; cedar ones sharpen cleanly, and basswood ones seem to fluff up. HB pencils are good for general marking out, whereas 2B are better for shading high areas that need to be shaved down.

Because of the constant need for resharpening in these projects, I have found a rotary pencil sharpener to be a good investment. And don't forget an eraser.

Strings, straightedges and rulers
It is useful to have a straightedge of 5 to 6 feet in length so that you can draw in guidelines or centerlines the full length of a paddle in one go. Long purpose-made straightedges are quite expensive, but I came by mine cheaply by searching through a stack of aluminum carpet edging strips and selecting a really straight one. It is also convenient to use a strip of wood if you can find a suitable one, and it is worth taking good care of it by storing it hung out of the way so that it doesn't get damaged or develop a bend. Drawing long straight lines can also be done with the aid of a string, and a useful string bobbin is shown on page 62. Use the stretched string to add a series of pencil marks that you can then join up with a shorter straightedge. Alternatively, use the string to snap on a chalkline.

A 30-inch steel ruler is good for

drawing in the shorter straight lines that serve as guides for rounding the shaft and carving the spine on the blade. The ruler should be as flexible as possible so that it can also be used for drawing in lines on the curved surfaces of the paddle. It seems a bit ironic, but the last thing most woodworkers use a ruler for is measuring. A ruler converts a dimension into a form that can be stored in your head, where it is rather susceptible to change. There is much less chance of error if you lift dimensions in a fixed form using a combination square or dividers. It is better still to use patterns or templates to store the dimensions permanently. Native canoe- and paddlemakers had such a system of comparative measurement, based on body dimensions like width of the thumb, span of the hand and the distance from fingertip to elbow. Undoubtedly, they marked important lengths on sticks too.

Except for the overall length, which clearly varies from paddle to paddle, all the dimensions for my paddles are stored on various templates and wooden blocks. For example, I have one piece planed to the starting dimensions of a shaft and another the size of the blocks that need to be glued on for a laminated grip. When I need any of these lengths, I simply lift down the pattern and mark off the measurement. Quick, easy and virtually error-free. On these patterns, I also

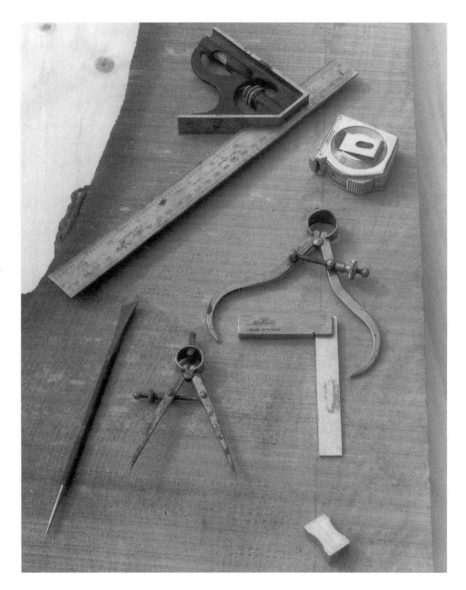

The main tools necessary for marking out a paddle: combination square, tape measure, calipers, scribe, square, dividers and pencil sharpener.

have the "overwidth" dimension marked, this being the final dimension plus ⅛ inch to allow for planing down to the required size. All these templates should be clearly labeled and kept together in a box so that they don't wander off or get used for firewood. Following the same idea, I have off-cuts of appropriate thickness threaded on a string—a sort of wooden feeler gauge—to take to the sawmill when I am choosing stock so that I don't make costly mistakes by bringing home wood that is too thick or too thin.

The paddle plans given in this book are in the form of offset tables that need to be plotted out as a series of points onto your wood or a template. These points need to be joined up using a flexible straightedge or strip. A 30-by-¾-inch piece of plastic laminate, such as that used for kitchen work surfaces, is ideal for most curves. A suitable strip can be cut with a router guided by a straight batten. For drawing very gentle curves, plastic laminate can be too flexible; a thin strip of a fair-bending wood such as spruce or pine is better. The long strip of laminate is also used for marking in lines on the curved edges of the paddle.

Carpenter's square

An interesting paradox: While there is a notable absence of right angles in a canoe paddle, a square is nonetheless a vital tool for the paddlemaker. Among other things, a square is required to check that the initial shaft section has 90-degree corners and to ensure that the blade pattern is laid out symmetrically in laminated paddles.

Despite its name, the combination square is not noted for its accuracy at setting right angles, and it is worth having a dedicated set square as well. However, a combination square is extremely useful for finding the center of paddle blanks, marking in the blade carving guidelines and generally transferring dimensions from one place to another.

A large plastic set square is needed for transcribing the paddle design from the table of offsets and for little routine jobs like checking that the bandsaw blade and sanding belts are set up correctly.

Dividers and calipers

Dividers have already been mentioned for lifting dimensions. Calipers (external type) are needed to check on the thickness of the blade as you slim it down from the blank. To get access to the center of the blade, you will need calipers of up to a 5-inch jaw depth. Store dividers and calipers fully open so that springs are not straining, and put a spot of oil on the threads from time to time.

French curves

A set of plastic French curves is nearly essential for marking out the tight curves of the grip and blade tip. Plastic laminate will snap if bent this much.

Spray can and plastic strips

A neat way of marking out the lines that indicate the final thickness of a blade is to attach a plastic strip of the required width with masking tape and then to spray with an aerosol paint can. The wood that needs to be removed gets painted, and the rest doesn't, because the strip shields it. Suitable strips can be cut from a roll of plastic damp-proof coarse material using a sharp knife (carefully) and a metal straightedge. This is a bit tricky to do, but once you have made the strips, they should last forever.

CLAMPS AND HOLDING THINGS STEADY

It would be difficult to design an object that is less suited to being held captive on a workbench than a canoe paddle. At the start of the project, clamping is straightforward, but as the paddle progresses from initial oblong sections to fluid curves, the problem becomes more severe and ever-increasing ingenuity is called for. You will need only one or two clamps when making a one-piece paddle, but a considerable number if your paddle is to be laminated. Rub a candle on clamp heads and bars from time to time to prevent glue from sticking.

G-clamps

From 6 to 10 clamps are almost essential for laminating the shaft of a paddle efficiently. The jaws of the clamps have to be sufficiently wide—6 inches is about right—to span not only the strips that make up the shaft but also the flat beam to which they should be clamped, as well as the softening blocks that must be inserted to prevent the clamps from damaging the wood. Such clamps can also be used for laminating narrow blades, but bar clamps will be needed for wider ones.

Crocodile clamps

These relatively inexpensive clamps are useful for holding one end of your long straightedge when marking out and for clamping splined blade-tip assemblies in place. They should be easy and quick to operate one-handed. It is useful to test this in the shop before you buy. I have seen clamps with springs that were so strong that they wouldn't have been out of place in a bodybuilding gym. Crocodile clamps can also be used in conjunction with bicycle inner tubes to hold together the strips while you are laminating a shaft (see page 64).

Bar clamps

Although complete steel bar clamps are available, you get a more versatile (and cheaper) arrangement if you purchase the clamp heads separately and make your own bars from 2-by-1-inch timber. I have a set of 18-inch bars that are ideal for paddlemaking.

Portable workbench

A portable workbench of the Workmate variety is suitable for building a paddle on, even if you have to put up with an accompaniment of squeaks and rattles as you work. The height of the bench is fine when you are sitting on it astride the paddle, but is rather too low to work on comfortably while standing. I have made an extension box out of ³/₄-inch block-board that clamps to the top of the Workmate and raises the working

height to a more comfortable 42 inches. The dimensions of the box are 18 by 12 by 12 inches.

Another solution to holding a paddle as you work is the classic shavehorse, in which the wood is held by a foot pedal. Making a shavehorse is an interesting project in its own right, and instructions are given in issue 90 of *Fine Woodworking*.

Vise

A large vise with wood-lined jaws is useful for holding the paddle steady during certain carving operations. You will need something immovable to fix it to.

Flat- and curved-sole spokeshaves and flat and curved cabinet scrapers are key tools for the fine shaping of a paddle.

TOOLS FOR CARVING

Coping saw

The easiest way to cut out the outline of the paddle is by using a bandsaw, although relatively few home woodworkers possess one. The job is perfectly feasible with a coping saw; it just takes a lot longer.

Smoothing plane

A 10-inch sole smoothing plane is a good tool for roughing out the paddle blade to approximately the correct thickness. A plane this size has a reasonable amount of momentum, which helps to stabilize the strokes.

Block plane

A smaller 6-inch block plane (the Record 60½ is a beauty) is excellent for taking the ridges off the shaft during the rounding process.

Spokeshave

The flat-sole spokeshave is the primary tool for the final shaping of the paddle. It is a beautiful tool; you have complete control over pitch, yaw and roll as you pilot it over the wood. The better types have knurled screws that allow for fine adjustment of the degree of the blade's protrusion. The tool is most often used by being pushed away from the user, but it can also be drawn toward the user, one-handed for very fine cuts, in a similar way to the traditional crooked knife. A minor limitation of this type of spokeshave is that the blade cannot easily get into the interior of tight curves, such as those around the throat of certain paddle designs. For this situation, the curved-sole variety can be used, al-though it is often possible to get by with a flat-sole spokeshave by advancing the blade a little.

A third kind of spokeshave, the curved-blade type, is excellent for carving the concave surfaces of double-blade paddles and for scooping out the wood, if required, adjacent to the spine on single-paddle blades. Unfortunately, curved-blade spokeshaves seem to be becoming extinct. A highly effective alternative is to grind the normal flat blade of a conventional spokeshave to a shallow convex profile. A jig for performing this operation accurately is described in *Advanced Paddlemaking*.

Drawknife

The drawknife is a folksy alternative to the plane and, to some extent, to the spokeshave. The developing paddle has to be held very firmly on top of an immovable workbench or table. If you haven't got a means of holding the paddle down securely, you are probably better off with a spokeshave.

Ax

This is the ancestral tool for rough-shaping a paddle and is still chosen by a few traditionally minded individuals. The rite of passage here is to be able to split a pencil line with your ax, something that must take a lot of practice.

Crooked knife

This is the tool that authenticates a "northwoods" paddlemaker. David Gidmark gives full instructions for making and using this classic item. They are also available commercially.

Craft/Stanley knife

A sharp Stanley knife is a good tool for quick removal of the overlaps of laminations at the throat and neck of the paddle, which otherwise seem to take an awful lot of sanding.

Surform rasp

The cylindrical type is the most effective for shaping grips. Interestingly, the Surform rasp was invented by noted English canoe designer Ken Littledyke.

Sharpening

Carving with blunt blades is a miserable business. It is physically harder work than with sharp tools, there is much more risk of gouging out lumps of grain, and all the charm of slicing off ribbons of wood is gone. It is well worth taking the time to learn how to sharpen your tools properly. For rehoning, you will need an oilstone, light mineral oil and a good book, such as *Tage Frid Teaches Woodworking*. A honing guide is a good investment until you feel confident enough to do without. When the dreaded day comes when the edge of a blade is so worn that rehoning is no longer sufficient, an electric grindstone, water-lubricated if possible, will be necessary to regrind the bevel.

TOOLS FOR FINISHING

Sandpaper and wire wool

Aluminum oxide paper is by far the best type of sandpaper that I've used. Even hand-sanding with this stuff is sufficiently rapid to allow you to keep well ahead of tedium. It makes wood seem almost like clay. This type of paper is also long-lasting and resistant to clogging. Sixty grade (60 grit) is excellent for initial sanding of the paddle after all the carving is complete, and 150 grade is good for smoothing off. I use 0000-gauge steel wool to apply oil (this combines oiling with fine "sanding"), although this is not suitable prior to varnishing because flecks of steel can get caught under the varnish and subsequently rust. Non-rusting bronze wool can be used instead, but this doesn't seem to have any advantage over fine sandpaper.

Sandpaper is applied in a variety of ways at different stages of making a paddle. When you are sanding the shaft, it should be held on a foam block, which helps to get smooth curves; when you are sanding the tight curves of the throat and grip, sand with the paper mounted on a shaped block that conforms to the contours of the paddle; sand the blade with a long, rectangular block that guarantees a flat surface and straight edges.

Cabinet scraper

A cabinet scraper is simply a small sheet of metal that is used to grate off tiny shavings of wood. It is a more modern version of the old piece of slate or glass, but there is still a satisfying traditional feel about using it. There are two types: flat and curved. The latter ("gooseneck") scraper is the more versatile and can be used both for finishing rough spots more quickly than with sandpaper and also for giving concave sides to the spine on the blade. You can find good information on sharpening scrapers in *Tage Frid Teaches Woodworking*.

Balance

I acquired an obsolete laboratory balance very cheaply, and it has turned out to be a real asset to my workshop. It is extremely useful for taking some of the uncertainty out of mixing glue, for building paddles to a specific weight if customers demand it, for calculating the surface area of blades (by weighing paper outlines) and for working out the shipping rate on outgoing paddles.

Use wood and foam sanding blocks to finish a paddle.

POWER TOOLS

Power tools are not necessary for making canoe paddles, but they come into their own if time or patience is lacking. They are nearly essential for the professional paddlemaker who has to work to the clock. The conventional wisdom is that they also replace the skill required with hand tools. I don't think so. It takes skilled and steady hands to control the wayward energy of power tools that can lure you on to making quite catastrophic mistakes almost at the speed of light. In this sense, using hand tools is easier; with them, it is quite difficult to write off a paddle with a single stroke.

A major downside of using power tools is that they reduce personal involvement—that intimate, firsthand control of the shaping process which is so appealing. Using power tools to cut out the basic shape of the paddle while using hand tools for the fine-shaping is a compromise that significantly speeds things up.

Bandsaw

A bandsaw is a big investment, but it is also an incredibly useful tool, especially if your paddlemaking is interspersed with carpentry about the home. A bandsaw, together with a thickness planer, forms about the most versatile combination that you can get, and you can recover the initial cost quite quickly with a few window and picture frames (if you need to justify the expense to your partner) and, of course, paddles. It allows you to cut the outline of the paddle in minutes and produce strips for laminated paddles, with the big

advantage that the cut edge is square. It is also easy to use the bandsaw to cut useful pieces of wood from timber that you have harvested yourself.

Choose a bandsaw with as simple and rugged a construction as possible, although this does not mean that it has to be big and heavy. I suggest that you steer clear of alloy models with pretty fiberglass panels, because there may be flex in the blade mountings that makes it harder to cut true. A saw with at least a 6-inch depth of cut is useful.

I have a little British-made Startrite 301, simply built from sheet metal and bar—the type of saw that is supplied to survive in extreme environments, namely school workshops. I go through two or three blades (three teeth per inch/skip tooth) a year, and it is worth keeping a small stock of these, because they tend to break unexpectedly in the middle of a job.

The bandsaw is the most domesticated of the power saws, a true gentle giant and much safer than a table saw, being relatively free from vices such as kickback. It is quite a compact tool and requires little floorspace, although you will need room to maneuver wood around it.

Saber saw

This is an alternative to the bandsaw for cutting the outline of the paddle. A powerful professional model is preferable to the do-it-yourself type, because the cut will stay square in up to about 2 inches of hardwood.

Table saw

This saw is a luxury item—nice if you have one. It finds specialized use in resawing stock boards and in cutting a slot in the tip of a laminated paddle blade for inserting a transverse strip, although there is another way of doing this job using a bandsaw. If you are thinking of buying a table saw, then a model with blade-depth and fence-adjustment facilities is worth the investment. I don't have these features on my saw, and I sorely miss them.

Belt sander

Another incredibly helpful tool, the belt sander is effective for fairing the outline of the paddle after cutting out with the bandsaw and for preliminary shaping of the grip. It can be used to sand the blade, but I prefer to do this by hand. Some models, such as the Elu (now DeWalt) MHB157, have a little detachable table that allows you to easily sand the square edges on the paddle prior to marking out the carving reference lines.

Drum sander

This is a specialist tool, an alternative to a belt sander, consisting of a drum about 12 to 14 inches in diameter driven by a powerful motor. The operator has a good level of control by guiding the paddle against the revolving drum. *The Wood and Canvas Canoe* provides instructions for how to make one.

Orbital sander

I've never used one on a paddle, but many people use them to fine-sand the blade.

Angle grinder

Again, I have never used this tool, but some woodworkers claim that it provides a quick method of grinding away excess wood. The thought of pulverizing wood in this way does not appeal to me; it leads too far from the level of involvement that I enjoy.

Thickness planer

An indispensable tool for making laminated paddles. Strips can be cut roughly to size on the bandsaw, then trued up on the planer. For this job, light alloy planers are ideal and are relatively inexpensive.

Hand-held power planer

This tool can speed up the rough shaping of the blade of a paddle to approximately the right thickness. Power planers are quite heavy, and it is all too easy to have one drop over the tip of the paddle blade and gouge out a chunk. A way around this is to cut the blade to size after you have thinned it down. In principle, a hand power planer can also be used to prepare strips for laminating, although I've never done this.

Electric drill

Your domestic power drill will take a variety of disks, drums and other attachments that can help in the sanding of your paddle. You get good control with a drum if the drill is held vertically in a stand. It takes a gentle touch to sand to a straight line or external curve, but it is easy to sand internal curves, especially if the diameter of the drum matches the curve you are sanding to. Drums are available in sets of different diameters. Pneumatic drums provide cushioning, which helps to produce smooth curves.

Router

This is an extremely useful tool in the general workshop but has only specialized application in paddle-making. Fitted with a rounding-over bit of the appropriate diameter, it can be used for the quick rounding of a shaft. I would recommend this only if you are in a hurry, because all you can produce are uniform, round shafts, and each expensive bit produces just one diameter of shaft, so you lose the flexibility of matching the shaft dimensions to the stiffness of a particular piece of wood. The router can also be used to inlay a decorative pattern of a contrasting wood.

If you are absolutely determined to use router technology in making your paddles, you will undoubtedly find a way. I heard of someone who routed a series of grooves in the blade region of the blank as an aid to carving. He went on to plane away the wood until he reached the bottom of the grooves, at which point the blade had flat surfaces and was of the required thickness.

Dust extractor

The fine dust resulting from power sanding, power planing and sawing of several types of wood is toxic, and measures *must* be taken to limit exposure. An efficient dust-extraction system is essential. Many vacuum extractors on the market can be hooked up to individual tools in turn and also used to clean up the workshop floor after a session to reduce the fire risk. You must also wear a dust mask specifically rated for toxic particles. Don't skimp on these measures.

HOMEMADE TOOLS AND JIGS

There is a fascination with making special tools and jigs that simplify otherwise complex tasks or sometimes just make possible things that you never thought you could do. Jigs often save much hard work, and there is some truth in the idea that the most inventive woodworkers are also the laziest.

It is possible, however, to take the idea of jig making too far. I once became bewitched by the idea of surrounding myself by jigs and sitting back and letting paddles almost make themselves. I spent considerable time making a sliding jig that enabled me to round a paddle shaft by using my router as a lathe. It kind of worked. It might even have been of some use if the shaft had turned out remotely straight.

Laminating beams

Thin strips of wood will conform to the shape of just about anything you clamp them to. It therefore stands to reason that you must have a perfectly flat surface on which to laminate the shaft of a standard canoe paddle, as well as some type of curved former for making a paddle with a bent shaft. You will need to find a 3-by-2-inch

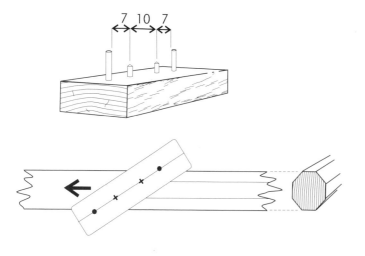

*Using a spar gauge to mark
8-siding guidelines on the shaft*

7　10　7

marks corresponding to the popular bent-shaft angles. In combination with this jig, I use my test paddle on which both the blade angle and shaft length can be adjusted. Once the desired angle has been arrived at by experimenting with the test paddle, the blade angle can be "programmed" into the jig.

Spar gauge

This is a handy gadget for marking out the carving reference lines for 8-siding the paddle shaft during the rounding process. For some mystical reason, pins spaced in the ratio 7:10:7 will scribe lines in exactly the right place. The gauge can be simple, using hammered-in nails with the heads removed and the inner two filed to a point; or complicated, with pencils replacing the inner two points. It goes without saying that the pins, or whatever, must be set in vertically.

Straight sanding block

Simply fix a half-sheet of 60-grit sandpaper to the bottom of a 10-inch length of scrap wood (about 3 by 2 inches). To make the block easier on the hands, use softwood and round off the top corners. Shallow grooves in the two long sides of the block help you to grip it. Bevel the front and back edges, and staple the sandpaper here so that the staples are neatly out of the way.

French curve sanding block

A pattern is given in the diagram for a "French curve" sanding block that is effective for sanding the tight curves of the grip and throat. The block was designed to take a

piece of square-planed softwood (it is less likely to warp than hardwood), 6 to 7 feet long, that has an absolutely flat surface. To this, screw four 3/8-inch plywood side pieces to create a right-angled edge to align the strips against (see photo on page 64). Give the surfaces that will come into contact with glue a good waxing with a candle to prevent the glue from sticking. Rewax often, and between making paddles, remove any little nubbins of dried glue that would otherwise prevent the next set of strips from lying flat. It is best to hang the beam when storing so that it doesn't bend or get damaged.

For making bent-shaft paddles, I have an adjustable hinged beam that I can set to any desired angle. It is simply a beam, similar to the above, but with a bridle joint about two-thirds the way along. The joint carries a bolt that is used to lock the two arms of the jig into any position. On the side, I have made strip from a standard sheet of sandpaper, which is held in place with hardwood wedges.

Foam sanding blocks

These are necessary for sanding curved areas of the paddle, where the foam allows the sandpaper to conform to the surface of the wood, and for general finish sanding. They can be bought or made from stiff foam packing. Ideally, use a very stiff foam for sanding the blade and a slightly softer one for sanding the tight curves of the shaft.

Blade-tipping jig

One way of strengthening the tip of a laminated blade is by letting in a spline (transverse strip) of hardwood. A good method for cutting the required slot is by passing the paddle blade, set vertically, over a table saw. It is rather difficult to hold the paddle so that the saw blade slices accurately through the rather slim paddle tip, and the consequences of having the saw misaligned are rather dire. Fortunately, it is simple to make a jig (see Chapter 5) that makes

the job much more controllable.

Plane a thin batten until it just slides along the fence groove in the saw table and its top is flush with the surface of the table. The fit of the batten into the groove has to be good so that it will slide easily, but there must be no lateral movement. If there is, the jig will be inaccurate. Next, screw this batten to a piece of plywood or fiberboard that extends beyond the edge of the table and beyond the saw blade (see illustration on page 84). With the batten in the groove, the board should slide smoothly across the saw table (with the blade retracted). Wax the batten, if necessary, to make it slide more easily. Make sure that the saw blade is set up parallel with the fence groove, and then carefully slide the jig past the blade so that the edge of the board is cut off. This cut edge now exactly aligns with the edge of the slot that the blade will cut in the paddle. The paddle can now be positioned accurately against the edge of the board so that the saw cut will pass exactly down the center of the blade tip. The paddle is clamped to the jig using a block, as shown.

This task, although straightforward, is nonetheless hazardous because the blade guard must be removed. Take extreme care. Do not do this job where unexpected distractions are possible. The setup shown in the illustration works well, and the clamps are used as handles to move the jig across the saw. If you don't let go of the handles, you won't cut your fingers off.

Full-size pattern for the French curve sander

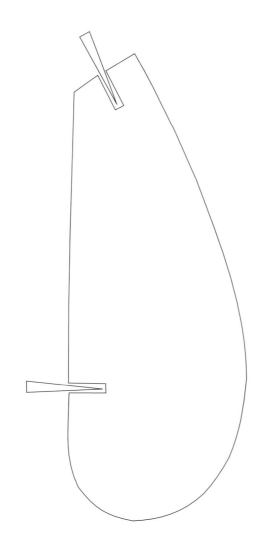

Paddlemaking Basics: Making a single-blade paddle

PREPARING A ONE-PIECE BLANK

Splits, knots and streaks

With the rigors of choosing the wood behind you, it is now time to relax and give some thought to how best to get a paddle out of the material at hand—a pleasant job to undertake over a cup of coffee. You want to plan the paddle to minimize the effect of imperfections in the wood.

The first concern is end checks. Because wood dries more quickly from cut ends, especially if they are not sealed with paint or wax, the material here shrinks more and splits usually form. Be careful—the cracks can penetrate considerably farther into the wood than is visible at the surface. Of course, you can play it safe and cut 6 inches or so from each end of the board, but that is wasteful. A bandsaw provides a foolproof way of removing all the cracked wood but a minimum of the sound material. Saw off just beyond the cracks visible at the surface, then cut off another thin sliver from the end—about $^1/_8$ inch wide, if possible. Flex this slowly but firmly. If there is any trace of a crack left in the wood, it will readily split in two; if it flexes but does not break, you have removed all the bad wood. Continue cutting off slivers until you get a favorable result.

Another concern is knots. At the lumberyard, you should have rejected wood with major knots, but it is worth having a closer look for little ones. Avoid any knots in the shaft—they interfere with the run of the grain and will significantly weaken the paddle. Small knots in the blade or grip region are structurally acceptable but will affect the look of the finished paddle. They may add interest, or they may spoil an otherwise flawless production. Getting a single knot central often makes it far more visually acceptable.

I have been plagued with dark streaks in ash. Sometimes they disappear as you carve; sometimes they get bigger; sometimes they just appear out of nowhere. As with knots, a dark streak can add interest or constitute a blemish, depending on your personal taste. I have found that some dark streaks harbor nasty little cracks, which spell the end of that particular paddle. Another pitfall that you will encounter sooner or later is embedded buckshot, with associated discoloration of the wood, which can be totally invisible from outside. It makes you wonder what else might be lurking inside the timber.

Coping with warped timber

Ideally, your timber will be straight and true. If it isn't, here are some ways of dealing with less than perfect material. Common ailments include boards bent along their length and twisted and cupped across their width. A thickness planer, if you have access to one, can effectively true up timber, but only hand-tool methods are described here.

Reject badly warped boards. A high degree of warping tells you that the board has severe internal stresses that may not have fully relaxed and so could cause problems later in the finished paddle. It might also mean that when the board is trued up, the grain will "break out" of the plane of the blank, a weak configuration. A piece with a minor bend or twist can be used—there is still a straight paddle in there somewhere—but be aware that extra work will be involved. A bent board must be thicker than the required paddle by an amount sufficient to compensate for the warp. Even

though it is easy to spot a moderately warped board, it is still worth checking an apparently straight piece with "winding sticks" — a pair of thin battens that you lay across each end of the plank — because these will highlight even a subtle twist. By sighting along the board, it is readily apparent whether the sticks are in line (the blank is true) or whether they are at an angle to each other, which means that the wood is twisted and remedial action is required.

Using a bent or cupped board

Mark a straight line (which is to become the centerline of the paddle) on one edge of the board, and then carry this across the two ends (having the ends sawn or sanded smooth helps here). Ensure that the lines on the ends are parallel. Finish by joining up these lines along the other edge. On either side of this line, mark out half the width of the paddle at a number of points, and join these up. Now

plane down to this straight slab marked out within the curved board, and continue as if you had purchased a straight piece in the first place.

Marking out a twisted board

Start by adding a centerline along one long edge of the board. Continue this line across one end on the parallel to the surface of the wood (that is, parallel to a winding stick laid on top of the board at

Truing up warped boards

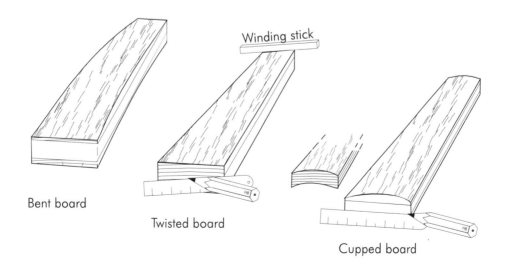

Bent board

Winding stick

Twisted board

Cupped board

that end). On the other end of the board, sight a ruler parallel to this winding stick, and continue the centerline. Finally, join up the end lines along the final long edge of the board. Mark out half the thickness of the paddle on either side of this centerline, as described in the last section, and plane down.

Marking out a bent and twisted board

The timber merchant must have seen you coming. Are you sure that you couldn't have found a better piece? If you are stuck with it, try a combination of the above.

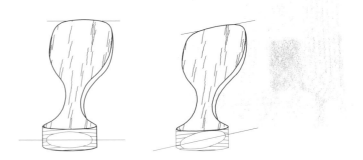

The grip and blade should be in the same plane

If the blank has a slight twist, the grip should be marked out with reference to the blade

MAKING A LAMINATED BLANK

Laminating a paddle blank from strips rather than using a single piece of wood has some definite advantages:

• Laminated blanks are normally absolutely true, because you will have (I hope) assembled them on something perfectly flat.

This saves much fussing during marking out.

• You will be able to make a quality paddle even if good pieces of wood are scarce. Many pieces of timber, even if unsuitable for a one-piece paddle, contain strips that can be successfully

incorporated into a laminated one.

• You will be able to amalgamate different woods and diverse grain directions to combine their desirable properties.

• Mixes of different woods can be used to considerable artistic effect. Although I personally dislike

Making both one-piece and laminated paddles is an economical use of stock

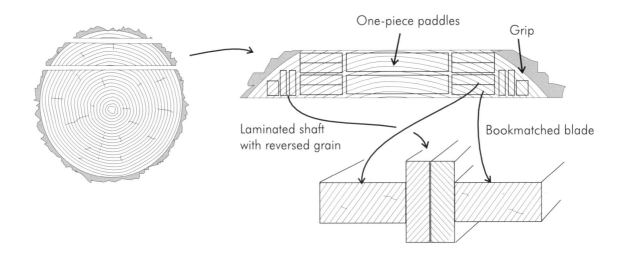

One-piece paddles

Grip

Laminated shaft with reversed grain

Bookmatched blade

the blatant "piano-key," light/dark/light/dark strips in many commercial paddles, more subtle combinations can be very pleasing to the eye.

There are disadvantages as well:

• It is hard to argue with the fact that you lose the simple beauty of a single piece of wood with a laminated paddle.

• Although modern adhesives are considerably stronger than wood itself, not all of them are suitable for making paddles, and they have to be chosen and used with care. A poor laminating job may result in a broken paddle.

Some purists dislike laminated paddles as a matter of principle, but I think they are both fun to make for a change and a good way to use up off-cuts from other projects (for example, making one-piece paddles). They are also a much more economical (and probably ecological) use of material than one-piece paddles.

It has been stated that laminated paddles are not flexible. This is simply not true in an absolute sense, although size for size, they may be less flexible than those made from a single piece of wood. It's difficult to make an exact comparison, because the properties of individual pieces of wood of the same species vary so much.

Composing the paddle

There are many different ways to configure the strips in a laminated paddle. Setups range from a simple three-piece (shaft and two blade strips) through to a multi-laminated paddle in which both the shaft and blade consist of a series of strips. In appearance, laminated paddles can range from very much the poor relations of one-piece paddles right through to quite stunning works of art. This difference is not so much a function of complexity but, rather, of the builder's flair in blending woods and grain patterns.

It takes a bit of experience to see at a glance the best arrangement for getting strips out of a board. With large boards resulting from cuts straight through the tree, it is possible to use the central portion, where the grain is likely to be flat, for one-piece paddles, and the sides (with angled or edge grain) for strips. Sometimes, a straight-grain piece is too narrow for a paddle but ideal for shafts. I like to cut these up right away into strips about $\frac{1}{4}$ inch oversize and hang them, clearly marked, for future use. In this way, by the time I come to use them, any twists will have come out. I make most of my laminated paddles by bookmatching the blade, which requires stock 3 to 4 inches wide but only about 1 inch thick. Bookmatching the blade

strips is definitely worth the effort if you have a bandsaw. The technique gives a mirror-image grain pattern on either side of center, at least on one face of the paddle. This simple expedient usually transforms what could have been a rather lackluster paddle into something quite special. Knots and other blemishes get mirror-imaged too, turning imperfections into features, but take care to get the features aligned across the blade.

When the wood in a blade gets wet, it gets slightly thicker. If different woods or different grain orientations are used in the blade, then individual strips can get thicker by different amounts and so stress the glue joints. The extent to which this can happen is very limited, because paddle blades are so thin, but when using a glue that is very inflexible, such as epoxy, you should take the precautionary measure of matching strips as much as possible on the basis of their expansions. Expansion data

Bookmatching

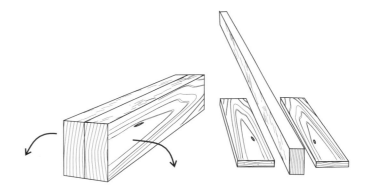

Cut stock board in half and
arrange either side of shaft to give
mirror-image figure

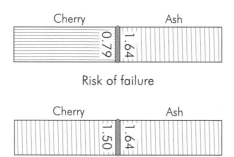

Risk of failure

Safe to glue

Use a string and bobbin to mark out a strip for a laminated paddle, above. The bobbin itself weights one end of the string, while the other is tied to a weight.

In laminated paddles, it is wise to consider expansion of the wood when it gets wet. The closer the expansion values are for the glued-up faces, the less chance there is that the joint will fail.

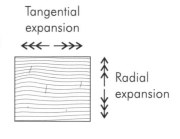

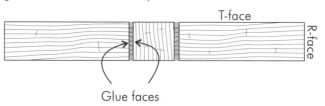

For a given wood, movement is greater for tangential (T) faces than for radial (R) faces. Faces with angled grain have intermediate expansion values

Glue faces

	Relative radial movement (R)	Relative tangential movement (T)
Ash	1.00	1.64
Basswood	1.36	2.00
Birch	1.57	2.00
Cedar	0.57	1.21
Cherry	0.79	1.50
Douglas Fir	1.00	1.57
Mahogany	1.00	1.43
Maple	1.00	2.14
Pine	0.43	1.29
Spruce	0.86	1.57

for common paddlemaking woods are shown in the table. You will notice from this that grain orientation is important, so you should consider this when composing your paddles. Based on the rarity of failure in laminated paddles, my guess is that this factor is likely to be important only in paddles containing strips with radically different expansions that are not completely sealed. If you laminate together

strips whose glued faces have broadly similar expansions (my rule of thumb is within 0.5), then you should be safe from this potential problem. Significant water ingress is likely only at the end grain of the blade tip if it has lost its protective coating of oil or varnish. Splining the tip of the blade may eliminate the problem by stopping splits from becoming established.

When selecting strips for color

contrast, remember that the oil or varnish you apply to seal the finished paddle will affect the tone appreciably.

Planing the strips

To produce laminated paddles, you need some way of cutting and planing strips. The ideal outfit is a bandsaw and thickness planer, which will make the process routine. Although it is possible to cut and plane strips by hand, this is a time-consuming business and requires considerable experience. You should be able to get strips cut and/or planed for you at a local woodworking shop, and since machine planing is a quick job, it should not be too expensive. The luxury of having your own tools is that you are free to change your mind at any stage and run up some new strips in an instant.

Strips destined to be laminated together really have to be square-edged; if they are not, you will glue up a whole heap of problems for yourself when it is time to mark out the paddle. Wood strips seem to have a natural tendency to turn rhomboid when they are planed. (I guess that if you wanted rhomboid, they would turn out square.) It is a frustrating experience to get to the stage of clamping the strips together only to find that they are not square-edged and that they arch rather than sit level. To give the strips the best chance of turning out square-edged, make sure that the table and blade faces from the bandsaw are used as the reference faces for the planer (see sidebar). If you need to do two cuts to bring the stock down to width and down to thickness, there is another little trick that you

should know to keep things square. Make the first cut on the bandsaw. Now turn the blade face downwards, and mark out the second cut on the upper face, the opposite face to the one just cut. This ensures that at least two faces of

the strip are at right angles and can be used for reference in the planer.

Preparing the strips for gluing

It is standard practice, when using a thickness planer, to wax the bed

---

Bandsaw and thickness planer

The powerful partnership between these two workshop heavyweights seems to make anything possible. They make cutting and planing one-piece blanks simplicity itself, and for producing laminated paddles, they are more or less essential tools.

A bandsaw has the innate quality of cutting perpendicular—but only if it is set up correctly; so frequently check that the blade is lined up at right angles to the table by using a plastic set square. Unless you have recently fitted a new blade, it is better to cut to a pencil line than to use the fence, because worn blades begin to wander quite badly as the set on the teeth begins to disappear.

It is important to remember that the saw and planer do work as a team; wood coming off the saw has to go into the planer in the correct orientation to preserve the bandsaw's accuracy. When you cut to a pencil line on the bandsaw, you have two faces at right angles: the reference (the lower or table face) and the face that you have just cut (the blade face). To preserve this right angle, remember to use these two faces as the reference faces (that is, the faces in contact with the bed) in the thickness planer.

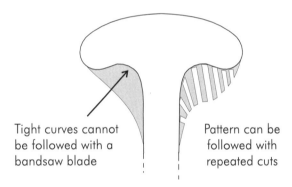

Tight curves cannot be followed with a bandsaw blade

Pattern can be followed with repeated cuts

Each bandsaw blade has a minimum turning circle that depends on the width of the blade and the degree of set on the teeth. The curves on some of the designs in this book (notably the throat and grip of the whitewater paddle) are too tight to be cut on a standard 1/2-inch blade, but the technique of kerf cutting can be used to get around this.

One school of thought holds the view that the surface of wood after machine planing is too smooth for maximal adhesion of glue. Proponents of this idea prescribe a light sanding to key the surface. I can see logic in this and it is easy to do, so I go along with it and lightly abrade the glue faces of the strips with 60-grit paper across the grain.

General considerations when clamping

Dry-clamping all the strips before gluing provides a useful rehearsal for the actual laminating process. I thoroughly recommend that you set up the complete clamping arrangement at this stage. It ensures that you have all the clamps at hand, and they will get set to the appropriate gaps. You will appreciate these time-saving details when you start to assemble the glued-up strips, at which stage the process suddenly becomes more stressful because you are conscious of working against the clock.

Don't get caught unawares by the tendency of glued-up strips to skate over each other because of the lubricating effect of the glue. The movement is due to the rotation imparted by the clamps, but it can be minimized by placing adjacent clamps in opposite directions and also by tightening all the clamps just a little before turning each one up to full pressure.

Another very good reason for alternating the direction of adjacent clamps is that they are heavy in a lopsided way and their weight tends to impart a twist to the paddle. This rotation is canceled out by having equal numbers of clamps pointing in either direction.

Top: Making a three-piece shaft on a laminating beam. The strips are aligned against edge stops screwed onto the main beam. The vertical clamps are bearing on a softening batten to spread out the pressure and are alternated on either side for balance. Above: An alternative way of clamping a shaft using inner tubing and crocodile clamps.

periodically so that wood slides freely through. I worry that a film of this wax might coat the strips I am planing and interfere with the bonding of the glue. To reduce this risk, I rub over the faces of the strips that will be glued with a rag dipped in methylated spirit (industrial alcohol), which is a wax solvent. The alcohol evaporates more or less right away and so doesn't itself cause a problem.

You do not want to build a defect into your paddle right from the very beginning.

Laminated shafts

It is easiest to construct a paddle around a one-piece shaft, but laminating the latter gives you the opportunity to build in some contrasting woods for artistic effect or to mix in some lighter woods to reduce the weight of the finished paddle. If you opt for a laminated shaft, then you will need to build the blank in two stages: first the shaft, and then add the blade and grip. If you try to do it all in one, you will be heading for a nervous breakdown.

Laminating a shaft is best done on a laminating beam—a precisely straight timber of at least a 3-by-2-inch cross section and a little longer than the paddle—fitted with edge stops against which the strips are aligned. This aligned side of the shaft becomes the reference face when truing up in the thickness planer. Make sure that the beam is well waxed to stop glue from sticking to it. I use a second straight batten, this time 2 inches by 2 inches, to sit on top of the strips to distribute the pressure of the clamps. The laminating beam must be straight, because any bends will be locked into your shaft as the glue dries.

Undoubtedly the most positive and least frustrating way to hold together the strips for a shaft is by using G-clamps spaced every 8 inches or so, with one at each end. The drawback with this arrangement is that it is quite expensive, especially if you are only going to make one or two paddles. A more economical alternative is to wind a bicycle inner tube around the strips or to use lengths of inner tube in conjunction with cheaper crocodile clamps, but these techniques only work if the strips are a really good fit to start with. I have heard of someone using a monster piece of heavy angle iron to weight down the strips instead of using clamps.

The strips that are going to make up the shaft should be at least $\frac{1}{8}$ inch overwidth to allow for truing up, but they should be planed to the final thickness before gluing.

When thicknessing the strips for a laminated shaft, plane the external strips in pairs so that, being equal in thickness, they give a symmetrical pattern on either side of the central core.

Clamping the blade

The typical way of securing the blade strips onto the shaft during gluing is by using bar clamps. Again, there should be a spacing of about 8 inches between clamps and one at each end of the blade. If you don't have enough large clamps, it is usually possible to cut away part of the outside strips near the throat of the blade to allow the use of smaller ones. Don't forget to wax the bars of the clamps periodically to prevent glue from sticking.

There is a considerable saving in both wood and carving time if the outer strips of the blade (the "wings") are made thinner than the shaft, although you need to be aware of the hidden consequences

Before adding the blade to a laminated paddle composed of strips of different thicknesses, the blade outline should be drawn on. To allow this, the strips are temporarily clamped with their top surfaces flush.

Panel pins are used to support thinner blade strips in position

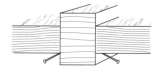

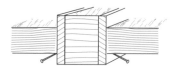

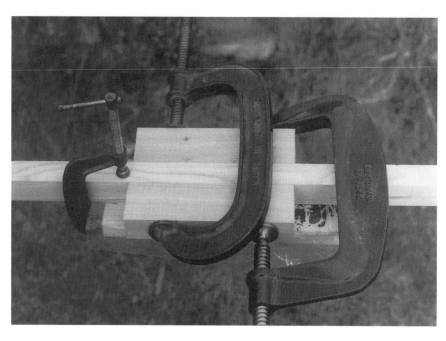

Clockwise from top left: Support the thinner outer blade strips by marking their position on the adjacent strips and tapping in temporary panel pins. The top part of the blade has been cut away to allow use of a smaller clamp. Clamps holding grip blocks face in opposite directions to prevent the shaft from twisting, and the shaft is supported to prevent sagging; grip blocks are supported on a block clamped to the shaft's underside.

of doing this. First, before the blank is glued up, the blade design must be marked out with the strips clamped with their top surfaces flush. Don't forget to do this, because afterwards, the blade faces are not flat, making accurate marking out almost impossible. Second, the thinner blade wings must be supported in position during gluing, because they cannot simply rest on the bar of the clamps as can full-thickness strips. Supporting

them is easy to do with ½-inch panel pins. Set the shaft on edge, and centralize the narrower strip by eye. Mark the position of the bottom of the strip with a pencil line, and tap in a panel pin near each end so that the heads are level with the line. These pins nicely support the thinner strips, although care must still be taken to ensure that the strips lie flush against the shaft and are not at an angle. The little holes left by the panel pins will be removed during carving. It is vitally important that the blade wings are positioned centrally so that the finished blade will be naturally aligned with the shaft. Care must be taken to ensure that they don't ride up when they are clamped after gluing.

Adding the grip blocks

The grip is formed by gluing two blocks (more in the case of complex or decorative grips) onto the sides of the shaft. These should be the same thickness as the shaft and typically about 6 inches long. The grip blocks need to be supported underneath in some way; I use a scrap of wood clamped underneath the shaft, as shown in the photo on page 66. I put a piece of plastic sheet on top of the scrap to prevent glue from sticking. A trap here for the unwary is having the shaft of the paddle bend under the weight of the clamps used to hold the grip blocks. This exerts leverage on the blade that can be sufficient to displace the strips. Be sure to support the shaft to prevent this.

Gluing up

Be careful to mix the glue in the proportions specified by the manufacturer. I keep my glue pot in a holder made from a heavy block of wood that prevents it from being knocked over. Make sure that you have mixed sufficient glue; few things are more infuriating than having to stop for a remix. Laminating a three-piece shaft takes about 30 grams of epoxy adhesive; adding four blade strips and two grip blocks takes about 25 grams. I find my old laboratory balance really useful here, because it enables me to mix any quantity of glue without having to search for suitable measuring containers, and formulation by weight is more accurate than by volume.

Glue all the surfaces to be joined, that is, both faces of each joint. Make sure that the faces are completely coated but not awash with glue; this is merely wasteful, as well as messy when the glue gets squeezed out and drops onto the floor. Woodworking clamps are rather efficient machines, and it is quite easy to overtighten them, squeeze out all the glue and get a weak, glue-starved joint. This is not just a theoretical possibility—it actually does happen. You should increase clamping pressure until glue just shows along the full length of all joints, and then stop. It is usually too dark underneath the blank to see this satisfactorily, so have a flashlight or inspection light handy. If the strips are not perfectly flat, you might have to apply a little extra pressure locally to get parts of the joint to close up; this is not ideal, but it is usually acceptable and should not overly compromise the strength of the joint as a whole.

This completes the laminating process. After a final, final check of the blank, I switch off the workshop light with a silent prayer that nothing will have come out of alignment by morning.

A basic three-piece paddle

This simple arrangement has a one-piece shaft with a wide strip glued on either side for the blade. It is the easiest type of laminated paddle to make. Extra blocks are needed as well for the grip, but the quoted number of strips usually designates the blade configuration and so does not include these.

Plane the shaft square-sided and

Suggested 3- and 5-piece lamination setups

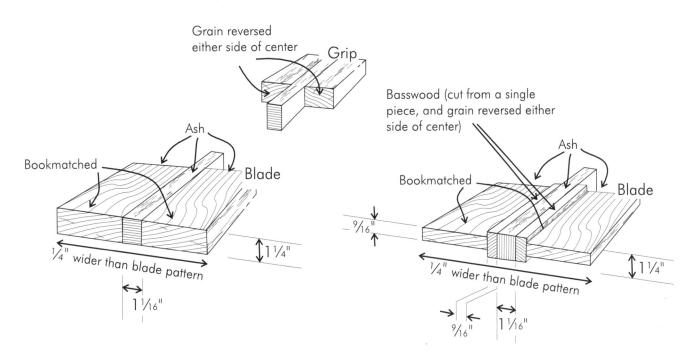

Grain reversed either side of center
Grip
Bookmatched
Ash
Blade
1/4" wider than blade pattern
1 1/4"
1 1/16"

Basswood (cut from a single piece, and grain reversed either side of center)
Ash
Bookmatched
Blade
9/16"
1/4" wider than blade pattern
1 1/4"
9/16"
1 1/16"

to its final dimensions before laminating. This provides a big saving in time compared with carving a one-piece, where squaring the shaft with a spokeshave is a lengthy step. The blade will look good if bookmatched from a single piece. It is best to have moderate contrast, either in wood or grain direction, between the shaft and blade.

If the contrast is too insignificant, the paddle might look a bit like an imitation one-piece; it is better to be up front and exploit laminating for its own sake.

On the other hand, if the contrast is severe, then the paddle might look too garish. If you have a piece for the shaft with the grain really well contained, then you can use it in either the flat- or edge-grain configuration. If the piece has some degree of grain breakout, it will be stronger used in the edge-grain configuration. The blade strips are better in the flat-grain orientation, which is more resistant to splitting.

A five-piece paddle

The five-piece configuration is one of my favorites. It gives an interesting effect without being overly complex or showy; and because the two strips next to the shaft are mostly encased, you can take advantage of some softer, lighter woods.

I make the internal blade strips a different width to the shaft. This looks better, less monotonous, to my eye. If I am using very contrasting woods—say mahogany against an ash shaft—then I make the internal strips very thin (around 1/4 inch). If I am laminating in a mildly contrasting wood for lightness—for example, basswood next to an ash shaft—the strips will be wider. It is a matter of some judgment to guess at the correct width of the light strips to counteract the normal tendency of the blade to be heavy and end up with a balanced paddle. It depends on the woods you are using, the blade design and the shaft length.

In the five-piece configuration, the blade wing strips can be quite thin, because they are set away from center, where the blade will be thinner. I have found that around 3/8 inch is about the minimum thickness I can get away with. I find it convenient to have the internal strips the same width as the shaft and to support the much thinner blade wings on these with panel pins during gluing, as described above.

These are just a couple of ideas. The beauty of laminating is that it gives almost endless scope for experiment.

Laminating checklist

◁ Compose the paddle.
◁ Cut and plane the strips.
◁ Degrease glue faces, if necessary.
◁ Abrade glue faces.
◁ Laminate and plane shaft (if appropriate).
◁ Do trial clamp-up of blade strips onto the shaft, with top faces
    of all pieces flush.
◁ Mark out blade pattern.
◁ Double-check length of paddle, and mark the position
    of grip blocks.
◁ Disassemble, glue up and reclamp.
◁ Check that all joints are closed.
◁ Double-check the alignment of all strips.
◁ Mark out grip when dry.

MARKING OUT

When you have a one-piece or laminated board planed to the thickness of the intended shaft (that is, the maximum thickness of the paddle), you are ready to begin marking out. Marking out a paddle is done in two stages. The first is drawing in the actual outline of the paddle, and the second is adding carving guidelines that help you end up with smooth and symmetrical curves. The second stage is done after the basic paddle shape has been cut out.

If you intend to work from an existing paddle, it is possible simply to draw around the blade and grip onto your board. This is likely to be inaccurate. Paddles do not lie flat and so are poor subjects for drawing around, and furthermore,

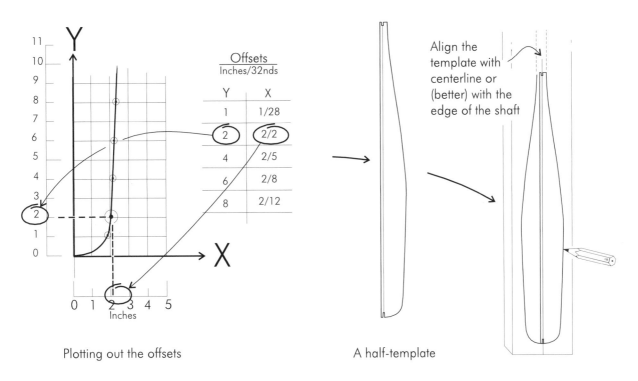

Offsets	
Inches/32nds	
Y	X
1	1/28
2	2/2
4	2/5
6	2/8
8	2/12

Align the template with centerline or (better) with the edge of the shaft

Plotting out the offsets

A half-template

Marking out the blank

you may find it difficult to get a truly symmetrical outline. Determining the exact centerline will not be easy either, and making a paddle with the shaft not centered on the blade isn't such a good idea. A much better plan is to draw around half the blade and grip onto templates, and then draw around these on either side of a centerline to ensure a symmetrical paddle outline. Thin plywood (¼ inch) is a good template material; hardboard (fiberboard) is also suitable, although the edges are easily damaged.

Basically, the same procedure is followed if you are starting from a design condensed into an offset table, such as the ones given in this book. Once again, it is far better to transpose the dimensions onto a

half-template first, because then you can check the fairness of the curves before you commit yourself to wood; and again, this method ensures a symmetrical paddle.

The offsets give the position of a series of points on the blade outline. The idea is to plot out these points and join them up to create the blade pattern. The individual points are specified relative to a reference point — the center of the tip of the blade. Each point is located by measuring its distance up the centerline from the tip (the Y figure) and out perpendicularly from the centerline (the X figure).

To make a blade half-template, start by drawing a centerline (the line that would pass up the center of the shaft) onto a piece of suitable template material. Mark on

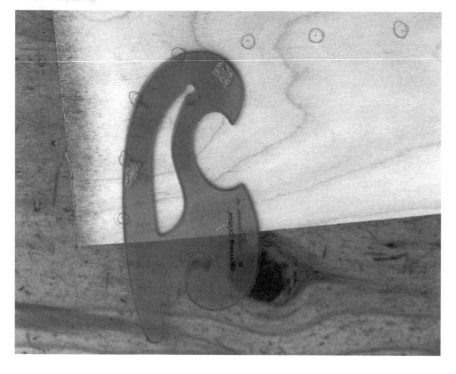

Top and above: Draw around a flexible strip of wood to join up the points of a blade design, and use a French curve to mark out the tight curve at the blade tip. Top right: One-quarter-inch birch ply is an excellent material for templates; notice the notch at centerline to help alignment.

this line the position of the tip of the blade. This point corresponds to Y=0 in the offset table. Starting at this point, mark off on the centerline the Y points along the length of the blade. At each Y point, use a plastic set square to draw a line perpendicular to the centerline. On each of these lines, mark out the appropriate X value measured out from the center.

When all the points are in place, join them up using a flexible strip. The method most often described for doing this is to fix the strip at one end using a panel pin at either side, and then flex the strip over the points and hold it in place with more pins so that you can draw around it. This works well for canoe sections, but it is not so good for the tighter sections of canoe paddles. I prefer a two-person approach, because this is a quicker way to get an accurate fit to the points. I flex the strip a pencil tip's width away from the plotted points, and then get someone to draw gently alongside the strip, being careful not to displace it. I find it easier to draw the curve in sections rather than to attempt to do it all at once. The curve at the blade tip is usually too tight to be drawn in easily with a strip, so I use French curves instead.

Cut out the template outside the pattern, and sand carefully to the line. It is worth taking considerable care to do this accurately, because any imperfections will be passed on faithfully to the paddle.

It is vitally important that the edges of the template are square; otherwise, the outline will be slightly different on each side, an effect that is more pronounced with thicker template material.

Finish off the template by making little saw nicks at the ends of the centerline to help with alignment, and then mark on details of the design and store somewhere safe where the edges will not get chipped.

Full-size patterns for grips are given on pages 144-145. To make templates from these patterns, first trace or photocopy them, attach the copy to the template material, and make marks through the paper with a sharp, hard pencil point every ¼ inch or so. Join up the points with a smooth line, using suitable sections from the French curves.

To transfer the design from the templates to the wood, first mark in the centerline on the top surface of the board using a long straightedge. Next mark the outline of the shaft. To ensure symmetry when doing this, set a pair of dividers to half the width of the shaft, and then mark this distance out on each side of the centerline. Now align the blade half-template with the centerline, and draw around this on either side of center. It is essential to get this right. If the blade is not symmetrical with respect to the shaft, the paddle may flutter in use because of unequal loading on either side of center. Finally, decide on the length of the paddle that you want, and draw in the grip using the appropriate template.

Clearly, the front and back of the paddle must be the same. If you are cutting and sanding the outline shape with power tools, which can be set to cut at precisely 90 degrees, only one side of the blank need be marked out. With hand tools, you will need to mark both sides, and it is vital that the centerline is accurately run around the blank and meets up with itself precisely. If this reference line is set up correctly, then the rest of the outline should match up on both faces of the blank.

DESIGNING YOUR OWN BLADE

After getting the feel for the performance of existing designs, you are almost certain to want to experiment with new ones to satisfy your own technical or artistic aspirations. In other words, it's fun. Here are a few things to think about.

If you plan to produce grips or blades with curves tighter than the "turning circle" of your saw blades, they will be much more difficult to cut out.

You can use existing paddle templates as "French curves" to produce new designs by incorporating sections of existing ones.

If you stray too far from blades that are 5 to 8 inches wide, 24 to 30 inches long and with an area of 120 to 160 square inches, you are likely to be disappointed with the results.

Scanning illustrations and manipulating the images on computer can capture paddle designs. More information on computer-aided design is given in *Making Canoe Paddles in Wood* and *Advanced Paddlemaking*.

CUTTING OUT THE BLANK

Laminated blanks are stable, and you can cut them out right away. If you are making a one-piece paddle, you should already have hung the board up for a couple of weeks and trued up any bends that have developed. It is a good idea now to cut out the blank roughly ¼ inch outside the line and hang it for another week. If you have a centerline drawn in, then it is easy to sight down this and spot any

warping. If the wood does bend farther, then you have a safety margin of wood to allow you to remark the pattern. After this hanging regime, it should be safe to shape accurately to the pattern line.

It is a rule in woodworking that you saw a little outside (at least ¹⁄₁₆ inch) of a pattern and then fair in to the line. This is a good principle to follow when cutting out a pad-

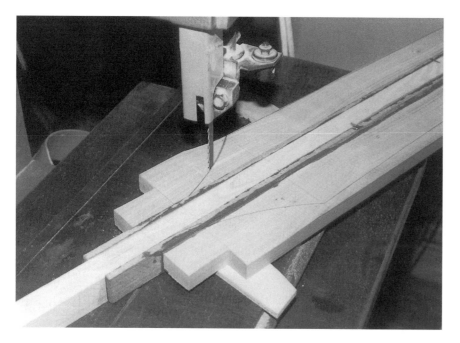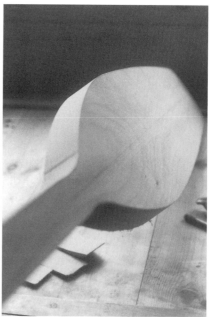

A bandsaw saves a lot of time when you are cutting out the blank. Cut outside the line except for the internal curves at the throat, shown above, because this region is difficult to sand. Above right: A cut and sanded one-piece blank. Sight along the blade curves to ensure that they are fair.

dle blank, except for the short sections of "internal" curve at the throat and neck. I have found that it pays to cut these regions accurately to the line, because they are quite difficult to sand. A lot of wood is removed during carving in these areas, and it is a simple matter to sand them smooth at the end. With laminated blanks, the shaft is already planed to the final dimensions before cutting out the paddle outline. You need to take considerable care not to cut into the shaft when sawing around the regions where the grip and blade actually merge into the shaft. This is an extremely easy mistake to make if your blade is even slightly off vertical, because the mishap will happen on the underside of the blank where you cannot see it. To avoid this, I steer the saw away from the pattern lines a little where they merge into the shaft.

Shaping the blank is easy with a bandsaw and belt sander, but quite a long job with a coping saw and spokeshave. At least using hand tools gives you time

to reflect on the joys of woodworking or on whether you really can afford a bandsaw after all.

Here is a tip for users of belt sanders. Different woods sand down at very different speeds. You can get a nasty shock if you are used to sanding a hard wood such as ash and you switch to a softer wood such as cherry or spruce. Using your accustomed sanding pressure, you can easily sand through the reference line before you are aware of what is happening. The same is true when you replace a sanding belt, because the new one will certainly have a much more aggressive action. You can exploit this by changing back to a used belt for finer sanding, but take care that the belt is not so blunt that it causes friction burns on the wood.

The shaft region of a one-piece blank is best faired using a spokeshave.

ADDING CARVING GUIDELINES

The next phase of marking out is adding the carving guidelines. These are pencil lines that show you where to cut to in order to get the intermediate shapes that lead to the final paddle. As your paddlemaking skills increase, you may find that you have less need for these aids; you might ultimately reach the point where you can visualize the paddle sufficiently strongly to be able to do without guidelines altogether.

There are two things to bear in mind with guidelines. First, once you cut them off, they are useless; you should normally work so as to keep the guidelines *just* visible. Second, removing guidelines once they have served their purpose can be a bother, so don't mark them in too heavily.

Blade thickness and edges

The first guidelines that you need to add are those that are going to tell you how much to thin down the blade and how thick the blade edges are going to be. To mark out the edges of the blade, it is necessary to establish another centerline, this time along the edge of the blank. This edge centerline is more of a concept than a reality; you don't actually want the line itself, only its position to work from. If you do go ahead and mark in this line all around the blade, you will only have to remove it again.

There are a number of different ways of marking out these guidelines onto the edges of a blade, the choice depending to some extent on what kind of shape your blank is in.

• *Combination square method* — for flat, machine-planed blanks.

• *Pencil-block method* — for sawn blanks with slightly rough or uneven surfaces.

• *String method* — for very uneven blanks.

• *Spray-paint method* — for any kind of blank, but especially suitable for laminated blanks with thin blade wings.

Whatever method you use, it is important to make sure that the blade edges are lined up with the shaft; otherwise, the finished paddle may look strange or exhibit bad character. Probably both.

Once you have marked in the blade-edge reference lines, it is a simple matter to work outwards from these to get the position of the blade-thickness guidelines.

Carving guidelines

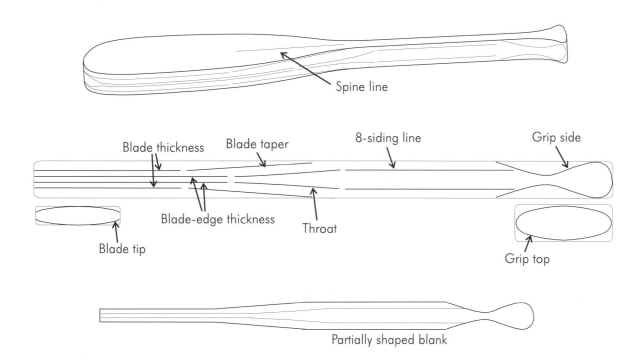

Spine line

Blade thickness   Blade taper   8-siding line   Grip side

Blade-edge thickness   Throat

Blade tip   Grip top

Partially shaped blank

The pencil-block method for marking out the blade-edge guidelines.

have a perfectly flat, smooth surface, such as a planed board or table top, somewhat longer and wider than the paddle blade. In this case, it is this smooth surface, rather than the face of the paddle blank, that is the reference for marking out. You also need shims of wood or any other convenient material for putting under a pencil to raise the point up to the correct height above the reference surface to scribe the lines. The way to proceed with this technique is shown in the photo at left. Finding or making the appropriate shims is the hard part; the rest is easy.

Combination square method

For a smooth, flat blank of uniform thickness (that of the shaft), marking the blade-edge reference lines is extremely straightforward. Set a combination (sliding) square to a depth a little under half the thickness of the blank, and draw in a short section of line from each side. These two trial lines are automatically centered on the edge of the blank. Adjust the combination square until the gap between the two lines is equal to the blade-edge dimension that you want. This is normally around $1/16$ to $3/32$ inch. Once you have the setting correct, run the two lines around the blade. The blade-thickness guidelines are easily added by repeating the above procedure, working to a dimension of $1/4$ to $3/8$ inch.

Pencil-block method

If the surface of the wood is even a little rough, then you cannot use the face of the blank as an accurate reference for marking out. For the pencil-block technique, you must

String method

If the blank is more uneven and will not sit firmly on a flat surface, it is difficult to use the pencil-block method effectively. Try the string method instead. To do this, set the paddle blank on edge and stretch a string along its length, centered above the shaft. This is best done by attaching the string to G-clamps fixed to the work surface at either end. Sight vertically down from the string, and mark a number of points along the centerline. Next, measure out from each of these points half the intended blade-edge thickness on either side. Join up these last two sets of points with your flexible strip of plastic laminate to give the blade-edge lines. The blade-thickness lines are added in the same way. It is quite tricky work, but the quality of the finished paddle depends on care at this point.

Spray-paint method

This radically different way of marking out the edges of the paddle blade uses not pencil lead but

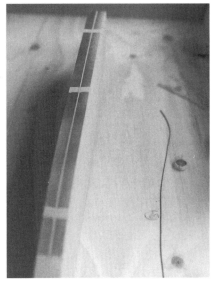

paint. Nor does it mark the wood you want, but rather the material that you need to carve away. The reference lines are automatically removed as you work, leaving you with little tidying up to do when you have finished shaping. The method is independent of any external reference and can be applied accurately to the roughest of blanks. The catch is that a paint spray can is more expensive than a pencil. Also, positioning the strips does require a fair amount of care.

The basic idea is this: you attach a narrow plastic strip around the edge of the blade and spray with the color of your choice; when you remove the strip, the (unpainted) reference line boldly stands out. The act of stretching the strip a little as you attach it helps to get it straight. To mark both of the required reference lines, you will need two strips: one the same width as the intended edge of the blade; and the other equal in width to the overall thickness of the blade.

Plastic damp-proof coarse material is a good source of strips, cut out along a metal straightedge

Clockwise from top left: The spray-can method — a plastic strip the same thickness as the required edge of the blade is taped to the blank; after a light spraying, the strip is removed, leaving an unpainted stripe that forms the blade-edge guideline. The blade-thickness guideline is added using a thicker strip; this strip is centered on the blade-edge guideline. The small notch in center of the strip is used for positioning, and a laminated blank shows the blade-edge and center guidelines sprayed in different shades.

with a sharp craft knife. This is a fiddly job, but it doesn't really matter whether the edges of the strips are a little bit wavy, because the edges of the blade will be trued up at a later stage anyway. While you have your tools out, it is worth making a set of strips for the common edge thicknesses that you use. For the edge lines, it is possible to use string instead of plastic strip, especially if you want to create very fine ($\frac{1}{16}$ inch or less) edges. The problem with string is that the width of the resulting line depends on the angle at which you spray, so you must be careful to keep the spray directly over the string.

To ensure that the plastic strips are straight and lined up with the shaft, stretch a string along the length of the paddle, centered on the shaft, and mark half a dozen points along the centerline of the blade edge. These provide reference points for positioning the strips, which need to be placed centrally over these marks. Starting at the tip of the blade, center the edge-thickness strip and hold in place with a narrow piece of masking tape. Next, stretch the strip very slightly, and align with the set of points; then tape in place, under a slight tension. You do not want to paint the edge at the tip or at the throat, because special templates are used here, so cover these areas with tape. The final job is to check that the strip is actually straight; it is easy to get it just a little crooked, even when carefully following the above technique. Check for straightness by viewing along the strip and also by holding a straightedge against it and gently pushing into line, if necessary.

Spray evenly in one smooth pass with the can about 1 foot away from the strip. Avoid overspraying, because paint can creep in behind the strip. It is easiest to spray the paddle if it is clamped vertically in a vise, but remember to mask off the vise and bench with newspaper. Peel off tape, carefully remove the strip, and *voilà*—a beautiful, straight reference line. A light spraying dries instantly, so waiting is not necessary. Repeat the process with the blade-thickness strip and a spray can of a different color.

The taper of the blade

A paddle decreases in thickness smoothly from the bottom of the shaft down into the blade, and guidelines will help here to keep things symmetrical during shaping. You will find that this is one of the easier tasks to do by eye, and you may want to dispense with these reference lines after the experience with making two or three paddles begins to develop your feel for the shaping process.

Grasp the blank as you would the finished paddle, and mark the position of your lower hand, top and bottom. Carry these lines right around the blank with a square. Set the blank on edge, and with the aid of a flexible rule or plastic strip, draw the tapering reference lines from shaft width at the bottom of the lower grip in to the blade-thickness reference lines at a position about one-third of the way down the blade. (I find it helpful to clip one end of the strip or ruler to the blank with a clamp when doing this step.) Ending the taper one-third of the way down the blade is just a ballpark sugges-

Mark in the blade tapering lines using a flexible ruler. One end of the ruler is pushed under a clamp to hold it in position.

Making flexible templates

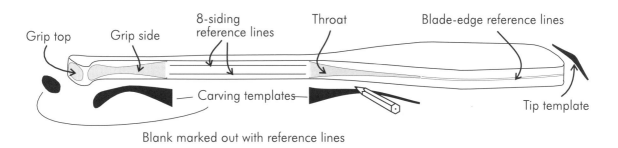

Grip top   Grip side   8-siding reference lines   Throat   Blade-edge reference lines

— Carving templates —

Tip template

Blank marked out with reference lines

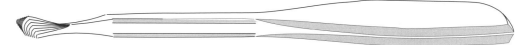

Blank carved to reference lines ready for final shaping

Lines to be added to curved surfaces are best drawn in using flexible templates. Patterns for these are given at the end of the book. To make templates from these patterns, first photocopy or trace them onto plain paper, then cut out outside the line. Fasten the paper pattern to a piece of suitable plastic sheet (from a plastic container or damp-proof coarse material) with paper clips or staples. Working on a scrap of wood, make holes with a scribe, sharp awl or pin through the pattern line and into the plastic every ¼ inch or so. The pattern is thus copied onto the plastic sheet as a series of holes. Cut out the pattern on the plastic by following the holes, dot to dot. It does not really matter if the outline isn't completely smooth, because these things get evened out when you sand the paddle. Finally, lightly scratch on the alignment marks, which help with the positioning of the templates.

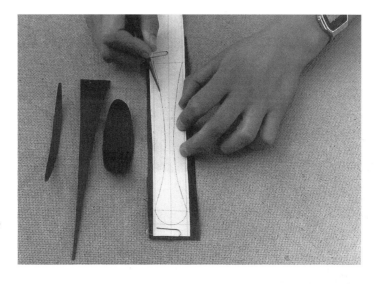

Right top: Tiny holes are scribed through the pattern into plastic sheet. Right: A grip-top template is cut out by following these holes.

Use a flexible template to add the throat guidelines.

tion. The length of the taper can be varied: longer for a stiffer blade and shorter for a more flexible blade. It is better to err toward the longer side, because you can slim the taper down if the paddle turns out a little too stiff but you can't do the opposite.

In the case of a laminated blank in which the blade strips have been made thinner than the shaft, these tapering guidelines are all but impossible to mark in, so the shaping has to be done by eye.

The blade tip

To increase abrasion resistance, the tip of the blade is often left a little thicker than the rest of the edge. But make it too thick, and the blade will produce a noisy plop as it enters the water. I use a template made out of plastic sheet to mark on the tip profile. The designs of these for various paddles are given in the plans section at the end of the book.

Marking out the throat

Clearly, at some point at the top of the blade, the edges have to be merged into the shaft. Getting a smooth transition here is not easy purely by eye, but it becomes quite straightforward by following suitable guidelines. In some paddles, this transition is rather abrupt; in others, it is smoother and more flowing.

I prefer the latter, because I think it makes a paddle look more elegant, although the former gives a slightly lighter paddle. Ideally, the edges should not start to widen out before the normal submersion point of the blade; otherwise, the paddle will unnecessarily catch water when sliced.

I tape the top end of the throat template halfway down the lower grip region and align the other end with the blade-edge reference lines.

Marking out the grip

The grip requires three guidelines to be drawn in: the front profile, the side and the top. The front will already have been marked (and cut out) as part of the overall paddle outline. The subsequent guidelines are drawn on the curved sides of the grip using flexible templates. A line should be drawn across the top of the shaft with a square to allow alignment of the template on both sides. The top template should be aligned with a centerline.

Tapering the shaft

If you decide to make a tapered shaft, the shaping must be done before you can add the guidelines for rounding the shaft. I like to taper the shaft from elliptical at the lower grip region to round just below the grip. To mark out this taper, set a pair of dividers to the width of the shaft (side-to-side dimension). Move the dividers around to the side of the shaft at the neck, centralize them (this is easy by eye), and mark off. Run lines from these marks to the full depth of the shaft at the top of the lower grip region. Carve to these lines with a spokeshave.

Guidelines for rounding the shaft

This is the part of paddlemaking that perhaps looks the most difficult to the beginner but is, in reality, one of the easier stages—provided that the guidelines have been accurately set up. For the marking-out methods to work, the shaft of the blank must have perpendicular faces, that is, have a square or an oblong section. The four corners of the starting section are taken off evenly, resulting in an octagonal section. The procedure is repeated, giving what is mathematically a 16-sided figure but is in practice so nearly round that a good sanding is all that is required to finish the process.

The techniques for creating the guidelines for the transmutation of square into round border on alchemy. It is not clear (to me) why they work, but they do. There are two methods: one using a graphical construction and the other utilizing a spar gauge.

The "square and diagonal" construction

Before you start, sharpen your pencil, because accuracy is important. Here is the basic technique. Using a square, draw a line across

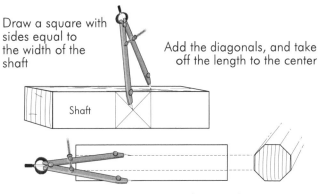

Draw a square with sides equal to the width of the shaft

Add the diagonals, and take off the length to the center

Shaft

Mark this distance from each side to give the 8-siding reference lines

the shaft. Next, set a pair of dividers to the width of the shaft, mark this distance off along the shaft from the first line, and draw in another at this point, again using a carpenter's square. You now have effectively drawn a square, the side of which is equal to the width of the shaft (see diagram). Carefully, draw in the diagonals. Now reset the dividers to the distance from a corner of the square to where the diagonals cross. It is worth checking this distance from all corners of the square. It should be the same. If it isn't, then you haven't drawn the lines accurately enough and should start again. When you are sure that you have the distance right, measure it off from one edge of the shaft—at each end—and join up with a rule (fixing the rule with a crocodile clamp helps). Do this again from the other edge, then repeat on the remaining three faces of the shaft. The dividers work some magic, and these lines end up in exactly the right place to indicate how much of the corners

have to be shaved off to reach the 8-sided stage. The method works for both round and elliptical shafts.

This basic technique is applied in various ways, depending on whether you want to carve a round or elliptical, uniform or tapered shaft. For a uniform shaft, the same length set on the dividers should be used on all four sides of the shaft. To produce an elliptical shaft, you need to do the "square and diagonal" construction separately on the top and side faces, which are of different width. For a tapered shaft, the construction needs to be done at each end of the tapered faces of the initial section.

Using a spar gauge

This little device, described in the "Tools" section on page 56, automatically puts scratch lines in the correct place for 8-siding as you slide it along the shaft. It works for both straight and tapered shafts. Although you can run the gauge down the length of the shaft, I think that it is better to use it just to mark out the ends and then join up these

The keys to paddlemaking

◄ Understand how to exploit the inherent accuracy of your tools.
◄ Break down the complex shape into simpler ones that you can carve accurately.
◄ The blank is symmetrical, just like the paddle that you are hoping to produce. So you don't have to create symmetry, but preserve it. Whatever you remove from one side of the blank, remove the same from the other.
◄ Recognize the best sighting points to be able to spot flaws.
◄ The most important tool for carving a paddle is not a spokeshave (or equivalent) but a pencil—for shading areas of wood to be removed.

marks with pencil lines, which are much more visible. A deluxe spar gauge, which adds pencil lines automatically, is described in *Making Canoe Paddles in Wood*.

This completes the marking out required at this stage, and all is now set for the shaping process to begin in earnest. The marking out of the spine has to wait until the blade is carved down to its final thickness. Some modifications to this basic scheme are required if you are making a double-blade or bent-shaft paddle, but these are considered later.

CARVING A SINGLE-BLADE PADDLE

If there is one thing that takes the fun out of making a paddle, it is having blunt tools. A blunt tool is tiring to use, it is likely to skate or rip the grain, and it does not give you that feeling of razorlike precision, of being in complete control. The first step in carving a paddle should therefore be to sharpen your blades; one sharpening should last for the paddle, except with very tough woods.

Another important consideration, which is often overlooked, is lighting. A well-placed light to one side will throw the surface of the wood into relief, showing up imperfections as clearly as craters on the moon. This is especially critical when cambering the blade. You should be able to see the flats cut by your plane or spokeshave, as well as the ridges that have to be taken off with subsequent strokes. Although it is pleasant to work outside under the trees in summer, the all-round lighting is

actually rather effective at obscuring the wood's surface. A garage, lit by a window at one end is a better, if rather gloomy, carving environment.

I recommend carving a paddle blank in the basic grip-blade-shaft sequence. The shaft is left with flat faces until near the end, because these enable the paddle to be clamped to the work surface while carving the blade. Once the shaft is rounded, the paddle is much harder to hold steady. Return to the blade again at the end to make final adjustments to the balance of the paddle.

Shaping the grip
The grip is first shaped down to the side guidelines. If you have a bandsaw, use this to cut just outside the lines, and then fair in with a rasp. Sight across the grip to make sure that you are taking the wood off straight across between the two sides. Even without a

  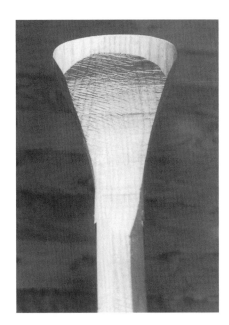

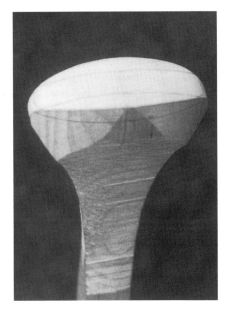  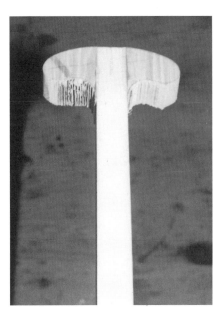

bandsaw, the shaping is still relatively easy with a just a Surform rasp or a mallet and curved chisel.

After the sides of the grip have been roughed out, move around to the top profile. I shape to this top guideline on my belt sander by gently rotating the paddle to and fro, taking care to keep the paddle shaft parallel with the surface of the belt. If you angle the paddle toward the sanding belt at this stage, you may remove wood that you didn't want to lose from the face of

Top, left to right: Cut to the side guidelines of the grip on a bandsaw, and shape the grip top on a belt sander. After shaping to the top guideline, the face of the grip should show a symmetrical curve. Above, left to right: The top of a grip is marked out with guidelines that help round

over the sides evenly. The edges are beveled between the lines, then sanded smooth; use sandpaper on a foam block to create smooth curves. The tight curves of the T-grip cannot be cut out directly on a bandsaw but can be shaped by kerfing — making repeated cuts in to the line.

Construction for guidelines for beveling the grip prior to rounding

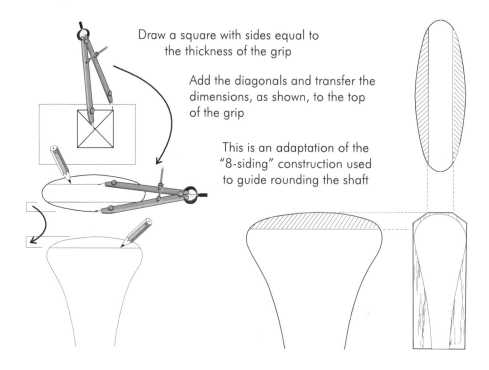

Draw a square with sides equal to the thickness of the grip

Add the diagonals and transfer the dimensions, as shown, to the top of the grip

This is an adaptation of the "8-siding" construction used to guide rounding the shaft

the grip. This job can also be done with a rasp or spokeshave. To speed up rounding over the top of the grip, I adapt the procedure (described on page 79) for 8-siding the shaft. By carrying out the same "square and diagonal" construction for the top of the grip, it is possible to add the required guidelines. Beveling off these sections (which again I do on the belt sander) saves considerable time with the subsequent hand-sanding.

A good way to smooth off the external curves of the roughly shaped grip is to use a 1-inch-wide strip of 60-grit paper pulled in a to-and-fro "shoe-shining" motion. I hold the paddle steady during this operation by sitting astride it on the Workmate, with a cushion for padding. It helps to continually change the orientation of the strokes. The faces of the grip are

best sanded with 60-grit paper on a foam block to remove the rasp marks. It is essential to protect yourself from the wood dust by wearing a suitable mask. The final job at this stage is to protect the grip from accidental damage with a piece of bubble wrap, or something similar, held on with a rubber band.

Carving the blade

The blade, being the business end of the paddle, is perhaps the most important bit to get right, because lumps and bumps may affect the paddle's performance, notably the stability while slicing, to a greater or lesser extent. One paddlemaker of note claims to be able to feel the effect of imperfections as small as one run in the varnish on a blade. These varnish runs must be something to behold! Carving a blade requires care but, because you have a network of guidelines to help you, not inordinate skill.

When shaping a blade, it is again convenient to work sitting astride the paddle. Have a 2B pencil within reach for marking areas that need special attention. Begin by roughing down to the blade-thickness lines. I use a smoothing plane for this, but some may prefer a power planer, and others a drawknife. It is easiest to start by taking a little off the edges and working in toward the middle; this way, the plane is always working on a convex surface. Repeat this over and over until you at last begin to approach the guidelines. Don't worry if you are working against the natural planing direction of the wood in some places; any pulled grain can be tidied up later. If you are new to planing, you will find out pretty quickly which of your muscles are being used. After the first few strokes, it can seem as though this stage will take forever, but you soon get into a rhythm, pausing only to clear the plane if it begins to skate, or to take in the aroma of the shavings that are steadily accumulating around you. You can also take comfort from the fact that each stroke of the plane makes your paddle about one-hundredth of an ounce lighter! In regions of the blade where you locally get down to the guidelines, mark the spot in pencil with a bold X to remind you not to remove any more wood. It is important to keep leaning over and checking how close you are to the guideline at the blade tip, because this is out of view as you work.

Locate bumps by running a

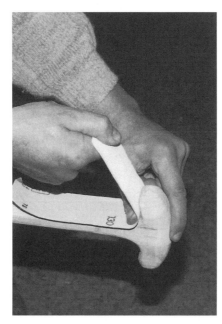

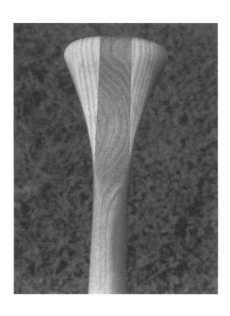

Top: Use narrow strips of sandpaper to sand tight curves on a grip. Center: Another useful sanding technique is pull-sanding. Press on the area to be sanded with your thumb while pulling the strip through. Bottom: A completed grip finished with oil shows two different tones of ash.

Splining a blade tip

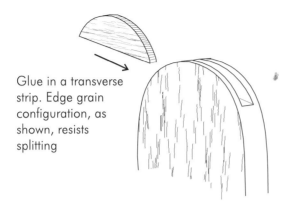

Glue in a transverse strip. Edge grain configuration, as shown, resists splitting

Splining the blade tip, above. Use of a jig allows accurate slotting of the paddle blade tip, into which the spline is glued. The clamps holding the paddle vertically in place also make good handles for running the jig over the circular saw blade, a hazardous procedure because the saw guard must be removed. Right: The transverse strip has been glued and is held in place with a crocodile clamp. The scraps help to distribute the pressure of the clamp.

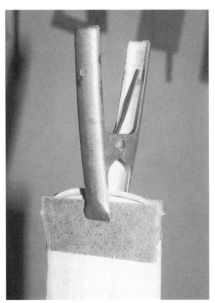

hand frequently over the blade surface; then mark the high spots with a pencil and shave off. You should end up with the blade cut down to the guidelines all around, on both faces, and more or less uniform in thickness across its width. Check this by laying a ruler on edge across the blade. There is a natural tendency for the blade to be a little thicker in the middle at this stage, but don't worry about this, because it is actually easier to bring it down to the final thickness when you start to do the cambering.

This stage of the carving process is quite forgiving, because a lot more wood has to come off later and mistakes can still be rectified. At the end of this phase, and it usually takes about an hour for a one-piece, the blank looks more like a paddle, less like a block, and you can detect the first stirrings of flexibility in the blade.

If you are making a laminated paddle, now is the best time to insert a transverse spline across the tip of the blade. A spline is a narrow strip set into the end of the blade that holds the laminations together; it is by no means essential, but it helps the blade to resist splitting. It can also be added after the paddle is fully shaped, but it is then harder to clamp the cambered blade. The spline should be an edge-grain strip of a strong wood such as ash, or you can use plastic laminate or aluminum sheet. Its width depends on the shape of the paddle tip and the arrangement of strips, but it should project at least $\frac{1}{4}$ inch into all the strips that it crosses. A jig for cutting the slot for the spline, shown in the photo on this page, has already been described. The spline is planed to be

The shape of the throat guidelines, far left. The paddle, left, is clamped at one end and braced against a wooden block at the other. This is an effective way of holding a paddle and provides good access to the shaft.

an easy fit in the cut left by a single pass of the saw blade. The slot can also be cut on a bandsaw, using a wooden block clamped perpendicular to the table as a "fence" to run the paddle along. Cutting the slot is quite demanding, because it has to be centered on the tip, which calls for some quite fiddly adjustments to the position of the paddle on the saw table. When gluing the spline in place, use a crocodile clamp with softening blocks at the very tip of the blade; if you position the clamp low down on the spline, the tip may gape open. When the glue has set, trim and sand the spline carefully to the outline of the tip.

It is now time to slim down the edges of the blade. To do this, it is convenient to clamp the paddle on its edge and switch to a spokeshave. I use the extension box on my bench to bring the paddle up to a comfortable height for work-

ing on standing up. The objective of this stage is to bevel the edges at about 45 degrees down to the blade-edge and associated guidelines (throat and tip). Get a feel for this angle. You can even spot-check against a protractor from time to time. The reason for cutting this bevel is that if you subsequently hold the spokeshave at less than 45 degrees when carving the surface of the blade, it should be impossible to cut into, and so ruin, the edge. Beveling is altogether more precise work, because it is possible to mess up with a single stroke. But it is quite easy to develop a mental approach that will make

Using a spokeshave

The spokeshave is a wonderful tool. It provides the link between the robust predictability of carpenters' tools and the light artistry of simple blade tools, such as the native crooked knife that David Gidmark describes in Chapter 10. It is almost impossible to use one without feeling the stirrings of creativity.

As with most blade tools, a spokeshave works best on a convex surface, because the pressure on the tool is concentrated on a narrow strip of wood. The carving routines described in this book attempt to exploit this fact. Try to keep an even pressure on the tool so that the shavings stay uniform in thickness, make your cuts as long as possible to avoid creating local hollows, and become proficient at using the tool both away from and toward you.

The short sole of the tool gives a rather minimal guiding effect. This frees up the blade to follow broad curves, but the tool is not effective in itself for cutting a flat surface in the way that a long-sole plane is. Yet you can use a spokeshave to create flat surfaces, such as the flats when 8-siding the paddle shaft, by following a simple routine. Bevel the edges of the surface to the guidelines that you are working to. The resulting ridge is lowered using the tool until the shavings just reach full width. Provided that you do not cut into the guidelines, you can hardly avoid getting a flat surface.

Using a curved-sole spokeshave is slightly different. You need to roll the tool over backwards and forwards to find the position where the blade bites, and then hold this angle as you work.

The tool's simple appearance belies its versatility. The following is a list of several ways in which it can be used. Hopefully, this will encourage you to explore the range of your other tools as well.

◄ You can get considerably more pressure on the blade if you "palm down" on one of the handles rather than hold them both in the standard fashion.

◄ To do curved cuts, for example around the tip of a paddle blade, keep one hand still and radius the tool around this with the other.

◄ Retract the blade at one side of the sole if you are working up to an edge that you don't want to remove.

◄ If you advance the blade slightly, this will enable you to work in tighter curves.

◄ It is possible to reverse the blade and use the tool as a convex cabinet scraper for scooping out wood next to the spine on a paddle blade.

A final thought—working on the sole with carborundum paper to create a really smooth surface makes the tool glide better on the wood.

Top: Shape the tip by "radiusing" with the spokeshave. Right: A spokeshave with blade reversed is used as a curved cabinet scraper.

this unlikely. First: Make each stroke a deliberate one; think about the track of the tool before you make the cut. Second: Be aware of where the shaving is coming off from the tool as it moves along; if the shaving gets too close to the guideline you are working to, angle the tool away slightly. These points, conscious thoughts to begin with, rapidly become instinctive as you develop the mental routines of making a paddle.

During the beveling process, I find it easier carving to spray-paint guidelines than to pencil lines, which is why I almost always use the spray-paint method for marking out. It is easy to judge how close you are to the line by the width of the paint remaining, and the job is complete when you just have a whisker of paint left. Whichever type of marking out you have done, stop when just outside the lines; the final truing of the edges is done later.

Now we come to the central issue of shaping the blade, creating a surface that has an even camber from side to side but is relatively flat from the bottom of the spine down to the tip. The area around the spine is shaped later and so is only roughly cambered at this stage.

The edge guidelines enclose the area you need to carve but do not tell you how to shape it. Here, the shaping is controlled not by working to a line but by following a routine with the spokeshave. Building this routine into your head is the key to cambering accurately. There are three general things to remember:

• Try to do full-length strokes as far as possible; the surface of the

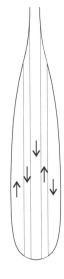

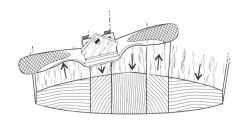

The natural planing direction of strips usually varies in laminated paddles

Because of the convex surface of the blank, it is quite easy to plane adjacent strips in opposite directions

blade will then stay relatively even.

• Start off at the side of the blade with the spokeshave less than 45 degrees to avoid cutting into the blade edge.

• Give the same number of passes to equivalent areas on the right and left sides of the blade face; this will help to keep things relatively symmetrical.

Another important factor here is the natural planing direction of the wood. In the roughing-down stage, this was ignored, but it becomes important now as the blade nears its final shape. If you run the spokeshave down the wood and you get a smooth zip, then you are going the right way. If you get a rough juddering and the surface of the wood pulls up, you are going the wrong way. If this happens, you must reverse the direction of the cut, and it is useful to become fluent in using the tool either away from you or toward you. The effect is intensified when you are shap-

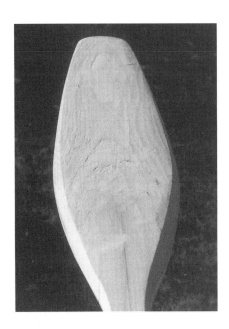

After the blade has been roughed down, above, the cambering process begins. Bevel the edges at 45 degrees down to the edge guidelines. This paddle has been roughed out against the grain, creating divots, but a careful spokeshaving in the opposite direction will correct these.

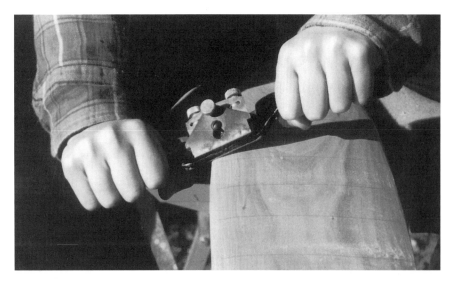

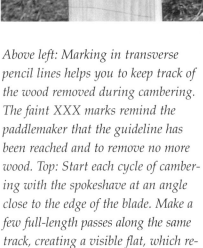

deliberate strokes along the same track, there should be a visible flat, especially if you have a light correctly positioned to the side. Catch the inner ridge of this flat, and continue with another set of strokes, with the angle of the spokeshave decreased slightly. This, in turn, produces another flat with another ridge to take off, and so the process continues. Using this basic procedure, work in toward the center of the paddle blade, decreasing the angle of the spokeshave all the while. On wide blades, it is not possible to get in very close to the center before the spokeshave becomes horizontal. Stop at this point—you will be able to work closer in to the center later in the process. On narrow blades, you should stop just short of the middle, by which time, the spokeshave should be nearly parallel to the blade surface. Now move to the far edge of the blade and repeat the process, working in toward the center from the other side. Next, turn the paddle over, and repeat the process on the other blade face to complete the cycle.

Now go back to the first edge of the blade, and begin the cycle over again. And so on. In time, the blade will develop a definite camber as each cycle takes off a layer of wood. When the camber forms, it becomes much easier to take off a few slices in the middle with the smoothing plane to thin down the blade a little. I also run the plane down the blade a few times at a shallow angle, on either side of center, to help flatten out any ripples that are forming during spokeshaving. When you are thinning down the blade in this way, it is important to plane equally on

Above left: Marking in transverse pencil lines helps you to keep track of the wood removed during cambering. The faint XXX marks remind the paddlemaker that the guideline has been reached and to remove no more wood. Top: Start each cycle of cambering with the spokeshave at an angle close to the edge of the blade. Make a few full-length passes along the same track, creating a visible flat, which removes a section of the pencil lines. Above right: The first cambering track.

ing a laminated blank, because matching the grain is often not compatible with lining up planing directions. In such cases, you must be prepared to reverse planing direction on adjacent strips. Fortunately, this is not as difficult as it sounds. It is useful to mark the planing direction on the strips with a bold arrow.

Begin by spokeshaving off the ridge of the edge bevel, with the tool angled somewhat less than 45 degrees. After three or four long,

Cambering the blade

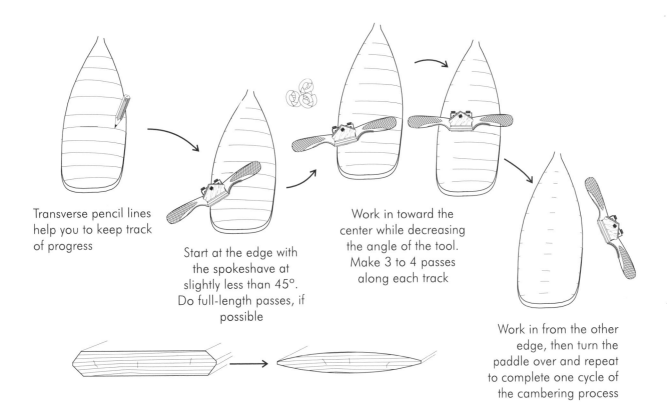

Transverse pencil lines help you to keep track of progress

Start at the edge with the spokeshave at slightly less than 45°. Do full-length passes, if possible

Work in toward the center while decreasing the angle of the tool. Make 3 to 4 passes along each track

Work in from the other edge, then turn the paddle over and repeat to complete one cycle of the cambering process

both faces (that is, top and bottom) of the blade; otherwise, it may lose its symmetry. Check at the tip reference line to make sure that the thinning process is not lopsided. After the blade has reached the desired thickness, stop the spokeshave cycles progressively farther out from the middle.

A simple trick to help you with this spokeshaving routine is to draw a series of transverse pencil lines across the blade, as shown above. This makes it easy to follow the progress of the spokeshave, since you remove sections of the pencil line as you go. When the line is removed in to the central section, you have completed that particular pass of that side of the paddle. The lines need redrawing for each new pass. This technique is useful to get you started, but you can dispense with it when you feel confident that you are in control of the cambering process.

Periodically check the blade thickness with calipers as you work toward the desired final dimension. Remember that the blade may thin down an extra $1/32$ inch during the subsequent sanding.

This is a rather stylized account of shaping a blade, and it is unlikely that a blade at this stage will have perfectly even surfaces. As the blade is nearing completion, the system tends to break down a little and you may have to go "freestyle" to cope with any local irregularities. The best tools for finding these are your hands; gently run them over the surface of the wood. Deal with any high

Clockwise from above left (directions continue from those in the photo caption on page 88): Move in toward the center of the paddle blade to the next section of pencil lines, and decrease the angle of the spokeshave slightly. Continue the process until the spokeshave is just short of center and almost horizontal. Repeat process from the other edge of blade, then repeat once more on the blade's other face, which completes one cambering cycle. Repeat cycle until the required degree of cambering is achieved. Check the camber with a straightedge, and periodically measure the thickness of the blade with calipers.

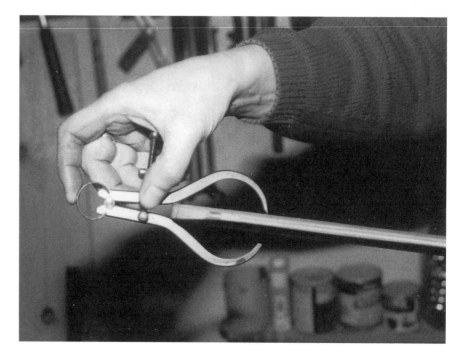

spots in the usual way until you are happy with the result. A factor that can interrupt the smooth flow of the cambering technique is a small quirk in the grain that causes the grain to pull locally and create a little depression. The best way to solve this is to stop the spokeshave just short, skip over and resume on the other side. Usually the spot can be smoothed out by a little stroke of the tool in the reverse direction.

You should, by now, have just about the blade thickness and camber that you want in the region of the blade below the spine. The camber should look symmetrical on either side of center, an impres-

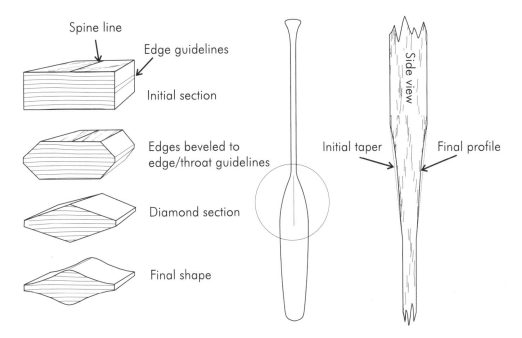

Stages in shaping the spine

Spine line

Edge guidelines

Initial section

Edges beveled to
edge/throat guidelines

Diamond section

Final shape

Side view

Initial taper

Final profile

sion that should be reinforced
when you hold a straightedge
across it. If this is not the case, then
identify any high spots and deal
with them. But avoid doing too
much "local" shaping; otherwise,
you might begin to loose the symmetry you have been working so
hard to retain.

Shaping the spine

The main function of the spine
is to stiffen the blade and to avoid
an abrupt change in flexibility
between the shaft and the blade.
It can vary from a short bump to
a long, prominent ridge, depending on the design and thickness
of the blade.

The concept behind shaping the
spine is simple. Wood is removed
from either side of the centerline in
the upper region of the blade to
create flat surfaces down to the
edge, resulting in a diamond cross
section in this area. This section
can be cut easily and accurately
with a spokeshave. The faces of the
diamond are then hollowed out to
some extent to produce the final
profile of the spine.

Add a section of centerline to the
top half of the blade to act as a
guide in carving the spine. It is
useful to have the center marked
on the tip of the blade and grip so
that you can find the center of the
blade easily. I find that I usually
slim the spine down considerably
from my original estimate as the
paddle progresses and so have to
redraw the "spine line" several
times as I work in this region.

I find it useful to put in edge
marks along the spine line and
throat/blade edge in the region
where I will be working. It is then
a matter of shaving off the wood
until just the ends of these marks
are still visible, working down
until the surface is flat. Because of
the shape of the paddle, you usu-

Clockwise from above left: This photo shows the centerline ("spine line") and edge marks that make it easy to see when the tool is too close to the edges as you start to shape the spine. The paddlemaker has marked the planing directions as a reminder, because this piece of cherry has a complex carving pattern. Spokeshaving in the wrong direction can pull out large chunks of wood, which could ruin the paddle at this stage. Wood next to the spine can be scooped out with a gooseneck cabinet scraper.

ally find that you need to shave toward the shaft in these regions. Not infrequently, you have to plane toward the shaft at the edges but toward the tip next to the spine. Interesting. Repeat the technique for all four "quarters" of the blade. Sight up the blade by holding the paddle out horizontally by the tip. There should be a pleasing curve from the blade edge

in to the spine, and this curve should be symmetrical on either side of center.

Sight the spine from the side. What you are looking for here is a smooth transition from the shaft into the blade. I prefer a slightly concave spine profile, which gives a refined look. If the profile is not to your liking, plane or spokeshave down a little. Take off a little at a time, then sight again from the side. Make sure that the profile is the same on the two faces of the blade. If you do lower the spine, you will have to redraw the centerline, add edge marks and again shave the surface flat to the edge.

When you have gained some experience, you will probably want to test the flexibility of the blade by bracing the paddle against the floor and slimming down the spine until you get the minimum amount of wood (and therefore weight) remaining while retaining the degree of stiffness that you want.

The flat surfaces adjacent to the spine can be hollowed out slightly, if required, using a convex blade spokeshave, a convex cabinet scraper or 60-grit paper on a foam block.

The final job is to tidy up the crest of the spines, which are probably still quite ragged. My method for doing this is first to use a cabinet scraper, which gives sufficiently fine control to allow slicing right up to the spine line, and then to finish up with a stiff foam sanding block with 60-grit paper, which I run up and down along the side of the spine.

With the camber in good shape and the spine complete, turn back to the blade edges. I like to leave these unfinished while I do the camber, because this gives me some buffer against accidental damage. Working carefully with the spokeshave—as usual making long, even strokes as much as possible—take the wood right down to the guidelines. Highlight with edge marks areas where you are away from the line to make it easier to control the fine shaving required. I usually find that the region ½ inch or so in from the edge stays a little thicker than I want, so I pay special attention to these areas and pull off several full-length shavings from each "quarter." The technique for holding the spokeshave is a little novel here and involves hooking a couple of fingers on the far side of the blade to get leverage.

Shaping the shaft

Rounding the shaft itself is a relatively easy proposition, although blending it into the blade at one end and the grip at the other is slightly more demanding. I use the method shown in the photo on page 85 to hold the paddle while I bevel the shaft. I'm sure that clamping the shaft in a large vise would be equally effective, but I don't have one. Using my method, the paddle shaft is clamped at one end and braced with a wooden block at the other to prevent it from rotating as you push against it with the spokeshave. To get access to the little region under the clamp that you cannot carve, it is a simple matter to switch positions of the clamp and block.

Begin by spokeshaving off the corners of the oblong section of the shaft down to the 8-siding guidelines; I put in edge marks along

Use a foam block to start the final sanding of the spine region. The block is run up and down against the spine line, above. True the blade edges with a spokeshave, left. Press the tool hard against the edge of the blade using leverage from your fingers on the opposite side.

these lines to make this job easier. Work at each of these bevels until the wood is flat between the two guidelines. Sight down the shaft frequently to help spot any areas that still require attention.

The octagonal shaft at this stage is actually quite attractive, and indeed, some native paddles are octagonal for part of their length. This suggests that native paddlemakers rounded their paddle shafts by using the 8-siding

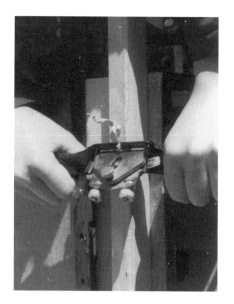

Before the rounding process begins, taper the shaft. Here, the tapering guideline has been edge-marked.

Blending the shaft into the grip and blade is easy if the guidelines have been set up properly

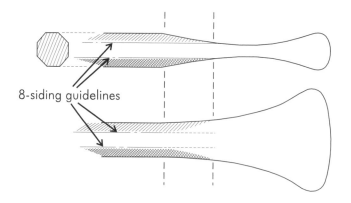

8-siding guidelines

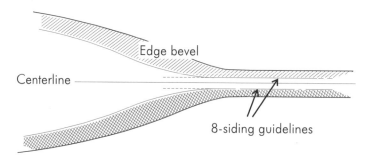

Edge bevel

Centerline

8-siding guidelines

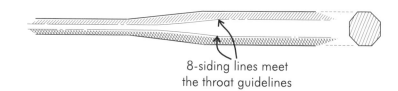

8-siding lines meet the throat guidelines

method too. However, in order to round the shaft, the corners again have to be taken off to reach the 16-sided stage. It is not necessary to draw in yet more guidelines to aid this process, because it is an easy job if you remember the following:

• Hold the tool at a "tangent" to the ridges, mid-angle between the face on either side.

• Do the same number of strokes on each ridge.

The resulting 16 faces of the shaft should be more or less the same width for a round shaft; the side faces should be a little larger than the top faces in the case of an elliptical shaft.

An easy way to take off the ridges is with the spokeshave. With a little practice and a firm grip, you will find that a neat way to do this is one-handed, pulling the tool toward you and getting tight, springlike curls of wood. Usually, in a one-piece shaft, four of the ridges need planing in one direction and four in the other. One day, I will work out why.

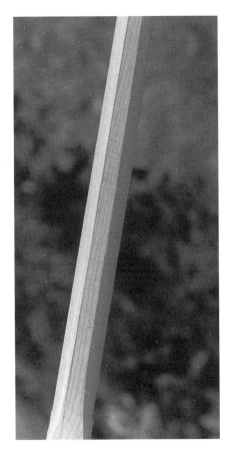

Be extremely careful to get the planing directions right to avoid pulling the grain, because any chips now are likely to show on the finished shaft. I find that six strokes of the spokeshave per ridge are about right, but let your eye be the final judge.

A minor problem with the spokeshave for this job is that it is quite easy to get a wavy finish because of the tool's short sole. Taking off the ridges with a block plane, which has a base of around 6 inches, consistently produces more perfectly formed shafts, but a different problem lies in wait here, because the grip and blade prevent access to the ends of some of the ridges. A good compromise is to use a block plane and finish off the inaccessible regions with your spokeshave.

With all the ridges taken off

Clockwise from above left: Bevel the shaft down to the 8-siding reference lines, then use a block plane to take off the ridges of the 8-sided shaft. Take the ridges off the ends of the shaft where the block plane cannot reach. The result: a 16-sided section.

Remove the ridges on the 16-sided shaft by "shoe-shining" with a strip of 60-grit sandpaper. The final flats on the shaft are highlighted with pencil shading, above right. These areas are blended by shoe-shining with a strip of sandpaper at a very shallow angle.

evenly, the next step is to sand the shaft to a fair round or elliptical section. This is best done using a 1½-inch-wide strip of 60-grit paper cut along the length of a standard sheet, exactly the same as was used for the grip. This strip is worked backwards and forwards along the shaft with a shoe-shining motion. I change to a different method of holding the paddle for this stage. The jaws of the Workmate are set with a gap of around 1 inch, and a sheet of foam is laid on top and pushed in between them. With a little adjustment of the jaw width, this arrangement holds the blade on edge quite firmly, and the "cling" in the foam grips the paddle blade when laid down flat. So the paddle can easily be rotated in 90-degree increments as I work on sections of the shaft as a sort of human lathe. I sit on a stool to the side of the Workmate and rest the grip of the paddle on my thigh. I haven't yet found a better way.

Start up the shoe-shining motion, and run the strip quite quickly along the shaft and back a

few times before rotating the paddle a quarter turn and continuing. Do the same number of passes for each quarter turn. I always rotate clockwise so that I don't lose track and compromise the symmetry that I'm after. Take care to keep moving back and forth along the shaft; if you dwell at any one place for too long, you will quickly cause a local thinning that will be all but impossible to remove and will be obvious when you sight down the shaft.

As you work, you will notice that the ridges round off very quickly and you are left with a series of flats, which wear away more slowly. In principle, when these flats disappear, the shaft is fair. However, when the flats have reduced to about ⅛ inch, an effective little "cheat" can speed up the process considerably. Apply pencil shading to the flats to make them more visible. Sight carefully against the light to make sure that you spot them all. Work at each of the flats in turn by shoe-shining with the sandpaper strip at a very shallow angle. You will see the

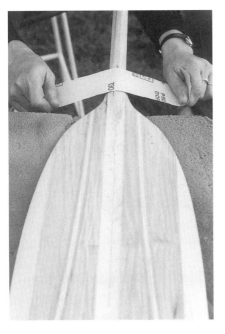

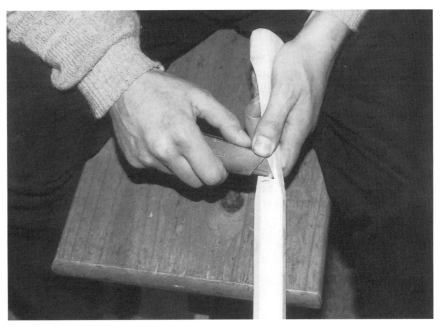

flats disappear before your eyes.

Finish off by using 60-grit paper on a foam block, running up and down the shaft in full-length strokes, rotating the shaft about an eighth of a turn after every few strokes. The foam should allow the sandpaper to conform to the curve of the shaft. This step removes the cross-grain scratches resulting from the shoe-shining. Continue with finer grades of paper until the shaft is smooth.

Final shaping at the neck and throat

The paddle is now approaching completion; it is definitely down-hill from here. One outstanding job is to blend the shaft into the grip at the neck and into the blade at the throat. This is done by shoe-shin-

Top left and bottom left: With a shoe-shining motion, move in from the shaft to the blade starting with the sandpaper at a steep angle that is progressively lessened. Top right and bottom right: Use the French curve sander to smooth the curves at the throat, and take off the lamination tabs at the neck with a craft knife.

ing with a strip of 60-grit paper, moving from the shaft out onto the blade or grip, decreasing the angle of the strip progressively to the horizontal as you go. Do one or two passes at a time, and then check your progress by sighting from various angles. In a very short time, these transition areas will be smoothly blended. The French curve sanding block is useful for finishing off the curves at the sides of the grip and throat.

For a laminated paddle, you also have to ensure that the edges of the strips (lamination lines) exposed at the neck and throat form smooth, symmetrical curves that match on either side of the paddle. I have suggested that you cut these areas a little wide of the outline to avoid cutting into the shaft. If you have done this, you will be left with little tabs of wood attached to the shaft. These are best removed using a craft knife, as shown in the photo on page 96.

Smoothing the lamination lines is done by returning to the sandpaper on a foam block. You soon get the feel for how a pass of the sandpaper alters the curve of the lines. If one section of the curve protrudes, a few passes will bring it back into line. Proceed cautiously, frequently sighting the lines from the top and the side. The pressure on the sandpaper from the foam as it conforms to the curve of the paddle naturally tends to result in fair curves, so you should find this job easier than you might have expected.

Finishing off the blade

With the grip and shaft complete, it is time to assess the balance of the paddle. It should balance an

---

Critical sighting points

Your eyes can quickly spot any places where the shape of your paddle deviates from a smooth, symmetrical outline. Some key sighting points allow you to spot flaws quite easily.

◄ Hold the paddle out by the grip horizontally at eye level toward a window in a dim room. Divots in the blade are revealed with brutal clarity.

◄ Sight down the shaft and rotate the paddle. This shows up undulations clearly. To feel for imperfections in the shaft, hold it in both hands and ratchet the paddle around.

◄ Look straight down the edges of the blade, and you will immediately spot any imperfections. The edges should be straight and of an even width.

◄ Sighting the blade tip full-on gives a good indication of how well the camber has been shaped.

◄ View the blade from the side. The upper and lower spines should be mirror images.

◄ Hold the paddle out by the blade tip just below eye level and angled slightly downwards. The curve on each side of the spine should be the same.

◄ Hold the paddle by the shaft, across the body, angled about 45 degrees downwards. Look at the curve made by the throat. Rotate the paddle slowly, which brings into relief the various curves in this region. There should be no bulges on these curves.

◄ To check the fairness of the curves, sight the grip from the top and from the side while slowly rotating the paddle.

---

inch or so up from the throat, but this is not possible for every one-piece paddle design. If necessary, thin the blade down a little more to remove weight, but keep an eye on the increasing flexibility.

Planing marks are best removed with a cabinet scraper. I use a straight scraper for the bulk of the blade, and a curved scraper for next to the spine. Scrapers are also extremely useful for final bits of shaping around the lamination lines.

The final shaping of the lower blade is done with 60-grit paper on a wooden sanding block about 10

inches long so that its long, flat face levels out local ripples on the blade surface. This is worked up and down the lower region of the blade, tilting it over slightly to follow the curve of the camber. As with all final sanding, this has to be with, rather than across, the grain so that the surface is not scratched. Be careful not to sand off the bottom of the spine. For a really flawless blade, spray the lower part, below the spine, very lightly with paint, and work at it with up-and-down (spine to tip) strokes of the sanding block until the paint just disappears. The sur-

face is then perfectly flat from top to bottom (but retains its camber side to side). To check the flatness of the blade between the spine and the tip, hold a straightedge against it—no light should show underneath.

Now for the trick that almost guarantees that you end up with perfect straight blade edges. Run the 10-inch sanding block along the edges of the blade in deliberate, continuous strokes. This flattens out any irregularities. Altering the angle of the block gives you control over the process. If you want to thin down the edges by a fraction, tilt the block a little and give a few more strokes. Finish off by giving the edges a very gentle sanding with 150-grit paper on a soft foam block to round them off slightly.

The area of blade adjacent to the spine is smoothed off with 60-grit paper on a foam block, and then the entire paddle is sanded with 150-grit paper, again on foam, always with the grain. All that is

needed to finish up is to give the entire paddle a fine sanding and sealing. These final steps are covered in Chapter 8.

The shaping of the paddle is now finished. It is the end of an intense relationship with the wood, a process of continuous thought rather than automatic action. As you make more paddles, you may find that there is a subtle shift in your thinking, from just anticipating using the finished paddle toward looking forward to the actual carving process. Take care—you are becoming addicted.

Left and center: The lower region of the blade has been lightly sprayed with paint and then worked with a sanding block. The low areas show up clearly where the paint has not yet been removed. Use an edge block to produce straight, even edges. Above: The result should be uniform edges that emerge gracefully into the shaft.

Adding Power:
The bent-shaft paddle

In addition to the obvious, the bent-shaft paddle is different in more subtle ways from a conventional one. Because of the bend, the paddle can be used only one way around; its geometry makes it very awkward for submerged recovery strokes. Therefore, the sections of the front and rear faces of the blade do not need to be the same.

Freed from this constraint, the paddle can make use of a more efficient flat power face, which is strengthened by an appreciable cambered face on the other side.

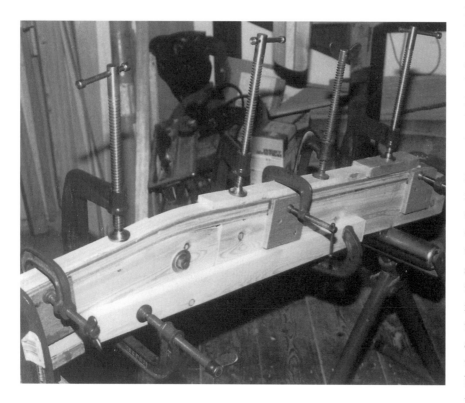

Laminating the shaft over an adjustable, angled former.

The shaft is typically a couple of inches shorter than the shaft of a conventional paddle. The grip is usually asymmetrical, with a pronounced bend that brings the plane of the grip back into line with the blade, which aligns it better with the hand. Bent-shaft paddles are usually quite stiff; there isn't much point in bending the shaft to increase performance, only to throw efficiency away by having flex in the structure. For this reason, the sides of the blade are not hollowed out in the spine region.

Making a bent-shaft paddle is really no more difficult than making a conventional laminated paddle. In fact, the greatest problem is deciding what angle to build into the shaft. You will need to make a special laminating jig to construct the shaft, but this is quite straightforward. I strongly recommend that you make a variable angle jig, as shown at left, because you can use this to laminate any angle of bend. This jig makes it easy to experiment; if your first paddle proves not to be quite what you wanted, it is simple to alter the bend by a degree or so and try again.

A thickness planer is a required tool for this project, as described here, although it would be possible to steam-bend the shaft from a single piece.

Making the shaft

I recommend making the shaft with seven wood strips of equal thickness. I usually alternate strips of ash and basswood to combine lightness with strength. The ash on the outside protects the softer basswood inside and stabilizes it against warping. It is vital that the strips are cut with the edge grain on the wide faces. Because the strips are so thin, flat grain is unlikely to be sufficiently contained.

Having so many strips means that a small change in the width of the individual strips has a big effect on the dimension of the shaft. If you try to plane the strips to a specific size (that is, the required shaft thickness divided by 7), you run a risk of the final shaft being quite a long way off the required dimension.

A better approach is to plane the strips a little overthick and home in on the required dimension by tiny increments. Reduce the planer setting by a fraction, and feed all the strips through again. Stack them together and test the thickness. Repeat until the stack of seven strips gives the thickness of

shaft that you want. At this stage, the strips should be ⅛ inch overwidth to allow truing up of the shaft after the glue has set. Because of the number of joints, laminating the shaft is quite messy—a lot of glue gets squeezed out—so it is a good idea to wear rubber gloves.

The technique of laminating the

described here, it will be in the order of 1 degree. The other consideration is the amount of glue to mix. For the 7-ply shaft described, I mix 60 grams of glue (resin plus hardener), which allows a small safety margin. There is quite a lot of gluing to do, so make sure that you can complete the job within

Arrangements of strips in a laminated bent shaft

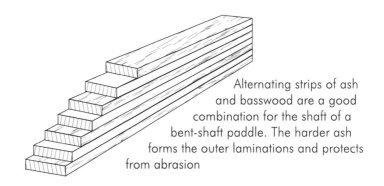

Alternating strips of ash and basswood are a good combination for the shaft of a bent-shaft paddle. The harder ash forms the outer laminations and protects from abrasion

shaft is basically the same as for a conventional paddle, with the exception that you need to allow a little for the relaxation of the laminations when the shaft is taken off the jig. To accommodate this, the jig must be set up to give a degree or so tighter bend than is required. Deciding on the appropriate relaxation angle involves a bit of trial and error, but for the configuration

the working time of the glue. It usually takes about 30 minutes. Add a fraction less hardener to the resin, if necessary, to prolong the working time of the glue.

At first glance, you might think that planing a piece of wood with a bend in the middle might be rather challenging, but it proves to be no more difficult than for a straight piece. Remember not to

Temporarily clamp the blade with the strips flush at the back surface of the blade (as seen above at the top of the photo) in order to draw in the pattern using a template. Then glue up the strips and clamp them with their surfaces flush to the bars of the clamps. This lower surface becomes the flat power face of the paddle.

wait until the glue has fully cured before you do the planing to protect the blades on your machine. I once jumped the gun and planed a bent shaft while the glue was still really rubbery. The shaft began to unbend noticeably while I was planing it. Surprisingly, after I clamped it back on the jig and allowed the epoxy to fully cure, the shaft was none the worse for the experience.

Adding the blade laminations

The power face of a bent-shaft paddle is normally flat. This fact makes the blade easier to shape than a conventional one. To set up the flat face during the laminating process, the blade strips are aligned to the bars of the clamps as a reference. The bars must be parallel; otherwise, the blade may well end up with a built-in twist. Sight across them to make sure of this.

Aligning the strips in this way leads to a well-camouflaged poten-

tial pitfall when you are marking out the blade. The natural impulse is to mark out the blade pattern on the flat face. Don't do this if you intend to cut out the blade using a bandsaw; you will find that it is not possible to cut around the line, because the shaft protrudes downwards, preventing the paddle from being slid across the saw table. You can mark out in this way if you are going to cut out by hand or with a saber saw. If you are going to use a bandsaw, then you need to temporarily clamp the laminations aligned on the non-power face while you draw on the pattern, as shown in the photo at left. When you have glued up the strips and realigned them with the bars of the clamps, the blade outline will be staggered across strips of different thickness; but I have found that this does not constitute a problem when cutting out.

When clamping the strips, take the trouble to get the power face of the blade as flat as possible to minimize the amount of planing that you have to do later. This point is worth special attention. Clamping is, in other respects, the same as for a straight-shaft paddle, except that the shaft will be protruding upwards and will require supporting. The grip blocks are added in the normal way. If you are making an asymmetrical grip, be sure to have the grip facing the right way, with the curve facing toward the flat power face of the blade.

This stage of laminating takes about 25 grams of adhesive.

Shaping the paddle

The bend in this type of paddle makes it harder to immobilize; I have not yet found a way of holding one fast on my Workmate when shaping the blade. An effective alternative is to clamp the grip end of the shaft to a long picnic-table-style bench and to put a foam-covered block underneath the blade to support it.

The shaft and grip are shaped as described previously. If you use the 7-ply configuration suggested here for the shaft, then you will get a welcome bonus when it comes to marking out the 8-siding reference lines. The glue lines separating the outer two strips more or less coincide with the position of the guidelines on the sides of the shaft, so you are saved the effort of working out where they should be.

In contrast to a conventional paddle, the blade-thickness and edge-carving guidelines are laid out by reference to the power face of the blade rather than to the centerline. This makes the job really easy: simply run a combination square down the edge of the blade. The tip and throat guidelines are added in the usual fashion, but the templates are of a different shape, reflecting the asymmetrical nature of the blade.

The flat power face should be nearly flat if the laminating has been set up properly. Sand smooth using a 60-grit sanding block or belt sander. My sander has a little frame attachment that prevents the corners of the belt from digging in. The remainder of the blade is shaped normally, except, of course, that only one face is cambered. The throat region cuts across several shaft laminations, so a degree of care is needed to get the glue lines symmetrical. The thickness of the

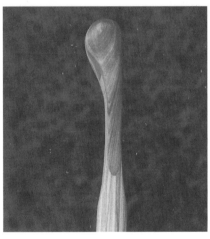

shaft laminations has been chosen so that two of them are approximately the required thickness of the center of the blade. Plane down the lower region of the blade until you just remove the third lamination (easy to spot if you are using a dark glue), and the blade will automatically be of uniform thickness. It is not usual to carve a spine on a bent-shaft paddle. The profile in the throat region is a modified camber, as indicated on the plan.

Bent-shaft paddles normally balance quite readily in the lower grip region.

Clockwise from top: Cutting out the blade – the blade pattern cannot be marked out on the flat power face because the angled shaft does not allow the blade to be cut out with the flat face uppermost. Next, the grip blocks are in position, supported on a scrap of wood. An extra central grip block is necessary to accommodate the curve of the asymmetrical grip on the bent-shaft paddle. Finally, the finished asymmetrical grip.

Twinning Up:
Double-blade paddles

Double-blade canoe paddles have a small but loyal following. They have some definite advantages, but there are some disadvantages too. When paddling with a double blade, you normally sit on the bottom of the canoe, so the boat is considerably more stable. Indeed, some canoe designs are so temperamental that they almost demand to be paddled in this way. It is possible to develop more power and a more symmetrical power output with a double- rather than a single-blade paddle, and so it is easier to make progress against a headwind. Paddling over the same course in the same canoe is up to 40 percent quicker with a double-blade paddle than with a single-blade one. But it is more tiring and not as much fun, because the nuances of single-blade use are largely lost. Double-blade paddles are good for shallow water, because they are used at a low angle and so have a small operating depth; but they are a hindrance on narrow waterways overhung by trees. Using a double-blade paddle is supposedly easier on a bad back.

The blades of double paddles differ quite radically from the single-blade type. As in the case of the bent-shaft paddle, the fact that the blades are unidirectional

A range of double-blade paddles

North Labrador Inuit paddle
with carved drip rings

Inuit paddle made for the explorer Gino Watkins in
the 1930s. It has morticed whalebone tips, nailed-on
bone edges and twine whippings for drip rings

John MacGregor's Rob Roy paddle of
1860s vintage with India rubber drip rings

A contemporary asymmetrical blade paddle:
the shape is designed to stabilize strokes by
equalizing the effective blade area either side
of the shaft when the blade is still partially
submerged (feathering not shown)

means that they do not need to have identical sections for the power and non-power faces. Accordingly, double blades take advantage of very efficient curved or spooned profiles, which provide further challenges for the paddlemaker. Even so, there is a system for carving such blades that allows you to stay in complete control.

Again because of the unidirectional nature of the double-blade paddle, there is more freedom in choosing the shape of the shaft. For the paddle described, I have selected an oval section, which is very comfortable to hold. The choice of length of double-blade paddle depends on the width of your canoe. You should be safe building a paddle in the 8-to-9-foot range; 8½ feet is good for my 32-inch-beam Peterborough. To maintain stiffness, the shaft has to be a little thicker than with a single-blade paddle, because increasing the length also increases the flexibility.

Many — but by no means all — double paddles have feathered blades. The purpose of feathering (setting the blades at an angle to each other) is to reduce the wind resistance of the blade that is out of the water. It is also an arrangement favored by slalom kayakers because of the reduced risk of hitting a gate. Use of a feathered paddle requires that the wrists rotate to bring each blade into play, and this is frequently cited as a cause of tendonitis, which seems to be a common problem. The standard feathering angle is 90 degrees, which requires an appreciable amount of wrist rotation. In an effort to reduce the destructive effect on the wrists but retain much of the benefit of feathering, an angle of 60 degrees is quite popular. Feathered paddles can be made with the blades in one of two orientations, the so-called right and left control configurations, named from the hand that stays fixed on the paddle. The choice is not re-lated to whether you are right- or left-handed but seems to be a matter of personal preference. It is commonly advised that you choose the right control orientation because this is more common, and therefore if you are swapping paddles, you are more likely to get one that suits you.

There is some debate over whether feathering is required at all for recreational paddles. The longer distances traveled when tripping mean that the paddle should be as kind as possible on the wrists, and there is no real advantage to feathering unless you are habitually paddling into a strong headwind. The Inuit "Greenland" double-blade paddle was traditionally unfeathered.

Joints are commercially available to allow double-blade paddles to be made in two sections; that way, the paddle can be taken apart for ease of stowage. Some joints also permit you to adjust the feathering angle. It should be possible to use such a joint to add on a grip to one section so that the paddle can be used either as a single or a double.

Construction details

Making a double-blade paddle looks like twice the work of making a single, but it isn't. The blades

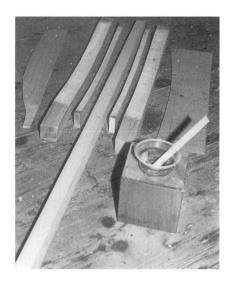

Shown above are the strips required to make the 5-piece double-blade paddle, together with the blade pattern and blade curve templates. Note the holder to prevent the glue pot from being knocked over. Right: A blade, cut and sanded.

Marking out and aligning strips for a curved blade

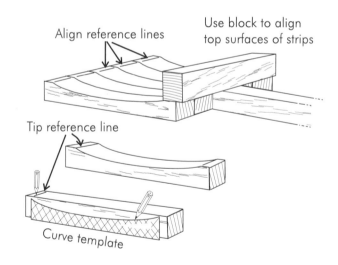

are smaller and need less carving, and you are spared the effort of making grips. Most of the shaping techniques are the same as those already described, so only the steps specific to the double-blade paddle will be detailed here.

The laminated paddle described has slightly spooned blades (with a simpler, curved-only option), which require a modified approach to shaping. The blade has three curves that you need to think about: top to bottom (the curve);

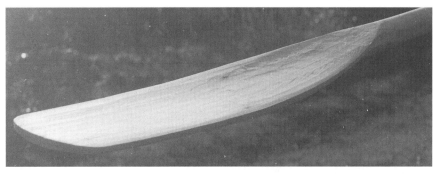

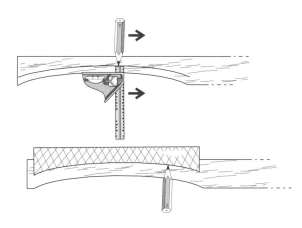

Two ways to mark out the blade- and edge-thickness lines for a curved blade

Clockwise from left: Cutting excess wood from the back of a blade greatly speeds up the shaping process. A blade is shown after it has been spooned with a curved-blade spokeshave. Smooth a curved blade with a sanding block cut to the same profile as the blade.

side to side on the power face (the spoon); and side to side on the back of the blade (the camber). The wood for the blade has to be the same thickness as the shaft to accommodate the curve, so it is not possible to use thinner outer blade strips, as can be done in a single-blade paddle. If you cut out the curve on the strips before you glue them together, it saves a lot of carving. Use a template to draw the required curve onto the strips; then all the curves will match, and

Using a flat-sole spokeshave for spooning a paddle blade

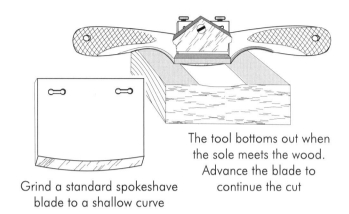

Grind a standard spokeshave blade to a shallow curve

The tool bottoms out when the sole meets the wood. Advance the blade to continue the cut

you will be left with a relatively easy job when sanding the blade surface smooth. To make the template for the paddle described here, transcribe the offsets onto plywood in the usual way. The curve is asymmetrical, so it is a good idea to mark the front (tip) onto the template. Align the template with the top (power) face of each strip, with a reference line marking the front edge of the blade. If you glue the strips together so that the top faces are flush (press a block against them to get them to line up) and the tip lines are aligned, then the curves on the individual strips should be in register.

If you are making a feathered paddle, the blades have to be laminated one at a time. A 90-degree feather angle is easiest, because you simply have to add the blades to adjacent faces of the oblong shaft. For other feather angles, you will need to plane flats at the appropriate angles.

For a paddle with a one-piece shaft and four additional strips

per blade, 35 grams of glue is sufficient. Once the glue has set, add the blade outline, cut out and sand to the line. If you have a small workshop, you will find it considerably more awkward maneuvering a double-blade paddle blank around than it is a single-blade one.

Whereas a straight blade is marked out for cambering by reference to the edge centerline, the reference in the case of a curved or spooned blade is the power face, so this has to be shaped first. To provide an accurate reference, the blade curve must be sanded smooth. If you are going on to make a spooned blade, only the perimeter need be faired, because the rest of the blade is going to be shaped further during the spooning process. For sanding, I recommend making a curved sanding block marked out using the blade-curve template; the block then conforms exactly to the surface to be sanded. Once the blade is fair around the perimeter, mark out the thickness of the blade-edge ($3/16$ inch recommended) and the blade-thickness ($1/2$ inch) guidelines using a combination square. Add the tip and throat guidelines using the appropriate templates.

By using the blade-curve template, the blade-edge and blade-thickness guidelines can be added without the need for fairing the blade, but I have found it more difficult to get accurate lines using this method.

If you have a bandsaw, you can save yourself a sizable chunk of time by cutting away the excess wood from the back of the tip of the blade, keeping a discreet distance outside the blade-thickness line. In this case, the blade width is limited by the jaw depth of your bandsaw.

The camber and spine on the back of the blade are shaped in the usual way, but the spooning requires a new and rather interesting technique. You will need either a curved-blade spokeshave or a flat-sole type for which you have ground a curve on the blade. The shaping technique described is for using the latter.

Draw a series of transverse pencil lines across the blade in the usual way to keep track of where you are removing wood. Start in the middle, with the curved blade of the spokeshave protruding only slightly. Make full-length passes, if possible (if not, then passes from the ends into the middle), down the center of the blade, in the same track, until the sole of the tool bottoms out and the blade ceases to cut any more wood.

Now work out from the middle, cutting equivalent tracks on either side of center, making three or four passes along each track, until you get to about $1/4$ inch from the edge. These outer cuts should contour the edge of the blade.

Stop at this point. Don't go right to the edge; otherwise, you will destroy the smooth curve of the blade profile. Return to the center and repeat the cycle over and over. As you proceed, keep advancing the spokeshave blade a fraction after every few cycles (because the blade will bottom out on the increasingly concave surface), stop a little farther in from the edge, and finish a whisker farther in from the tip. The operation is complete when you end up with the appropriate degree of concavity,

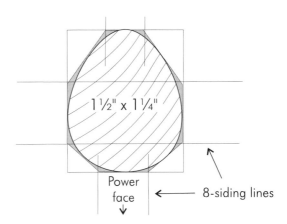

which you can determine by laying a straightedge across the edges of the blade.

If you opt to omit the spooning and shape your blades to a simple curved profile instead, you need only sand the power faces smooth with the curved sanding block. If the curved blade strips are well aligned, this is a simple job; if they are crooked, you are in for a long haul.

After final sanding and sealing, the only remaining job is to prepare for that particularly bad habit of double-blade paddles—dripping water into the canoe—by adding drip rings. A Turk's head is often used for this.

Having gained experience with a simple double-blade paddle, you will find that there is much to experiment with—different feathering angles, more elaborate asymmetrical blades and traditional Inuit designs.

When Wood Meets Water: Oil or varnish protection for your paddle

Bare wood exposed to repeated cycles of wetting and drying will almost inevitably develop splits sooner or later. It is important, therefore, to seal the surface of your newly made paddle to prevent (or at least minimize) water absorption. When it comes to sealing paddles, there are two rather polarized camps: the proponents of varnish and the followers of oil, with little love lost between them. Here are the selling points of the two types of finish.

Varnish gives a hard protective barrier that is virtually impervious to water as long as the surface is unbroken. Being itself a hard substance, varnish physically protects the wood from scratches in a way that oil does not. A varnish finish may last several years before it needs a major recoating, unlike oil, which needs recoating often.

Oil is much easier to apply and to refresh. It is even possible to carry out additional shaping after you have tried out the paddle. You can simply oil the newly exposed wood, and it will blend in perfectly. Oil gives the paddle a pleasant feel in the hands, and the surface is less likely to cause blisters. It imparts a silky sheen to the wood that doesn't mask the natural texture of the material; this is wood as nature intended. But oil does not provide an absolute barrier to moisture; some water can still (slowly) get in. More important, however, is that it can still get out. Water entering through a scratch gets trapped beneath a varnished surface and precipitates rotting. Blackened wood around scratches is a common sight on varnished paddle blades, especially if they are made of an absorbent wood such as basswood.

Oil has another advantage. An oiled surface breaks up the light and hides flaws, such as sanding scratches, as if by magic. Varnish seems to concentrate the light and highlight imperfections.

Both finishes will adequately protect your paddle, but one thing that the devotees of each school of thought will never agree on—and this really is the central issue—is which finish looks better. Oil gives a deep antique wood look; varnish is bright and clean and modern.

Prior to applying either type of finish, the paddle should be wiped over lightly with a damp cloth to raise the grain. After allowing the paddle to dry for an hour, give it a light sanding with 150-grit paper. Repeat this wetting/sanding routine a few times until the grain stops rising.

VARNISH

Producing a flawless varnish finish is not an easy task. It is an unforgiving process that will flaunt your mistakes—runs and brush marks—for all to see. But as much as any other part of making a paddle, it is a skill that can be learned and proficiency progressively acquired. The trick is to memorize what works and what doesn't. There is usually as much—often more—to be learned when things go wrong as when they go right.

Work to a system. Aim to make brushing a planned process, not merely a haphazard dabbing. Try to standardize the amount of varnish on the brush, use the same number of strokes per brushful, and employ the same pattern of brush strokes; you will then have more chance of developing a reproducible technique. Learn where the varnish collects, and use less varnish there; or check frequently for runs or pooling. Don't varnish near a radiator; this can cause problems due to premature setting. It is easier to avoid runs in the varnish by using more coats of thinned varnish rather than fewer coats of thicker varnish. Four coats of varnish thinned by the addition of 10 percent (by volume) of thinner gives an adequate protective layer. Thinning the varnish slightly also makes it easier to apply evenly and helps to avoid bubbles. Use the solvent specified on the can (some manufacturers don't recommend thinning their product), and mix by gently rotating the container, rather than stirring, to avoid introducing air bubbles. To achieve good bonding between coats, add subsequent coats within 24 hours, before the varnish has fully set. The depth of the shine builds noticeably as you add coats of varnish.

There is no definitive way for holding a paddle during varnishing. I support paddles horizontally on two blocks with a couple of small nails protruding. Having the paddle horizontal avoids most of the problem with runs, but one is left with the small imprints of the nail heads in the varnish. Another method is to drill a small hole in the grip and hang the paddle from this on a fine nail. The hole is filled after the varnishing is complete.

Dust is a major problem when varnishing. It appears out of nowhere the moment that you reach for the can of varnish, and with your mind bent on perfection, the evil strands seem to grow on the paddle like fur. A dust-free environment is a rarity in the average home, and most of us have to make do with varnishing in an out-of-the-way corner, preferably when the other occupants have gone to bed. Because most dust settles on the paddle from above, suspending a dust sheet over your work area is one way to reduce the problem.

A particular difficulty with laminated paddles is that varnish is absorbed to different extents by different woods. The result is that the surface builds faster on the less absorbent wood, and after the first couple of coats, the paddle can look disappointingly patchy. A combination of ash (mildly absorbent) and basswood (very absorbent) shows this effect to a marked degree. In this situation, the paddle should be given a good sanding with 200-grit paper to level the surface after each of the first couple of coats until the wood is completely sealed and the coats start to build evenly.

Several different types of varnish are classified according to their chemical composition. Traditional spar varnishes are based on oils and are generally quite flexible. Polyurethane varnishes, on the other hand, are relatively rigid. The wood in a paddle in use is constantly flexing and moving in response to changes in moisture content. There is the suspicion that since hard varnishes will eventually crack, a flexible type is probably the better choice. The downside of spar varnish is that it scratches more easily than polyurethane does. Some more esoteric concoctions are available that by clever chemistry might well achieve a better balance of toughness and flexibility, and these are probably worth seeking out.

The varnish should contain a UV barrier (most quality ones do) that prevents the light-induced breakdown of the polymer structure. Epifanes and Inter are brand names that seem to be reliable.

A question that you will have to resolve for yourself is just how good you want the finish on your paddles to be. Varnishing has a seemingly insatiable appetite for time, and it is debatable as to how much effort you should expend in getting a flawless finish on an object that is, after all, just going to pound rivers and lakes all day. The question is different if you are making your paddle for display, but I personally think that show paddles and canoes, built exclusively for looking at rather than for using, are rather sad and soulless. My feeling is that varnish finishes for working paddles should be professional but not obsessive.

Revarnishing

The tips and edges of the blade inevitably get scratched and worn. It is important to keep these areas sealed against water absorption with frequent touch-ups of varnish. When the paddle becomes sufficiently scuffed as to become an embarrassment, a complete revarnishing job is in order. Any loose flakes of varnish around scratches must be scraped off, and the edges of varnish remaining should be feathered. Then the entire blade (or paddle) must be sanded with 150-grit paper to key the surface. Clean with a rag dipped in methylated spirit, which will evaporate almost immediately. Finish off by applying several coats of varnish.

Revarnishing can be as quick or as time-consuming as you want to make it, from a simple recoating through to an elite job involving sanding down to the wood and essentially starting over.

OIL

In marked contrast to varnishing, applying an oil finish is (almost) simplicity itself. Oil is wiped on thickly and allowed to soak in, and then the excess is wiped off. It is a difficult job to botch. Follow only two rules: the surface must be kept wet (that is, loaded with oil) during the absorption phase, and all the excess must be wiped off before it sets to a nasty wrinkled gum.

Two common oils are used—boiled linseed and tung—either individually or as a mixture. Boiled linseed oil is perfectly adequate, although tung oil is reported to be more waterproof and to darken less with age. It is also considerably more expensive. Don't confuse boiled with raw linseed oil. The latter is not suitable, because it does not contain driers (added catalysts) and will set extremely slowly.

Oils dry by oxidative cross-linking of their component fatty acids; in other words, they need air to set. In a thick layer, the oil sets at the surface, creating a film that excludes any more air and therefore greatly slows down further curing. This is the reason excess oil must be wiped off. It also means that buffing up a newly oiled surface helps to set it by increasing the exposure to air.

Because oils set quite slowly, they have more chance to penetrate the wood than varnish does. Even so, the depth of penetration of oil is very small, usually less than a millimeter, except at exposed end grain, where liquids can penetrate more freely. End grain is exposed at the tip of the blade, which is fortunate because it permits more thorough impregnation there—just the place where protection is needed the most. Undiluted oils are quite viscous and do not penetrate the wood particularly easily. Penetration can be enhanced a little by thinning down the first coat with white spirit or by heating the oil before applying it.

Once oil has set on the wood, it prevents penetration of subsequent coats. That is why it is imperative that the surface be kept wet with oil during the initial coating of a new paddle to get the maximum amount of oil (and therefore protection) into the wood.

Here is the oiling procedure that I use, which was designed in light of the factors above. Very carefully (see safety advice below) heat the oil to just below the boiling point, and smear it liberally over the paddle with a brush. Hang the paddle up by the grip over some newspaper. The excess oil will collect at the tip and drip off—thus automatically keeping the tip wetted for maximum penetration. Inspect the paddle periodically over the next two hours, and recoat any areas that appear to be drying out, paying special attention to the top of the grip (where end grain causes rapid penetration) and also to any strips of thirsty woods such as basswood. After two hours, wipe off all excess oil with a rag or paper towel. The following day, apply a thin coat of oil using a pad of 0000-gauge wire wool (use a cloth on ash, because steel flecks get caught in the grain), leave for a few minutes, then wipe off.

A major advantage of an oiled finish is that it is immune to dust, which simply gets wiped off when you buff the surface. It would be hard to put too high a value on this benefit.

The tip of the paddle should be re-oiled frequently, preferably after each outing, after the paddle has dried out. It only takes a minute.

Safety Note

Heating oil is hazardous. There is a significant risk of it catching fire. Have a damp rag within reach to smother the flames. Do not drop oil on exposed skin—it will burn you. Wear eye protection. Destroy oily rags and paper, because these can spontaneously ignite with the heat given out during setting.

Re-oiling

One of the joys of choosing an oil finish is that re-oiling the paddle, either for a touch-up or for a total recoating, is so simple. Rub on a coat of oil, leave it for a couple of hours, then wipe off and buff the surface. Oil will penetrate where surface film is broken. Recoat the paddle at least every three months.

Compromises

In an effort to make varnished paddles kinder on the hands, a combination of oil and varnish is sometimes used—commonly varnish on the blade and oil on the shaft and grip, or all varnish except on the top of the grip. Occasionally, the top of the grip is left untreated to become impregnated with the skin's own oils. These compromises do work, although to my eye, a varnished blade combined with an oiled shaft looks a little odd.

Even though varnish and oil finishes are fundamentally different, a couple of compromises have been suggested in an effort to combine the good points of both. I haven't tried them, and so I cannot comment on their effectiveness,

only on their theoretical appeal.

One method is to seal the bare wood of the paddle with a coat of thinned-down varnish and then apply an oil finish. I feel that this procedure might still suffer from the disadvantage that water entering through scratches might be trapped and hasten rot.

An alternative is to use a resin-containing oil, such as Watco, Deks Olje or Cetol. These give a waterproof surface that is easier to apply than varnish and physically tougher than oil. Matt and gloss finishes are available, at least for Deks Olje. A homemade (and much cheaper) substitute can be made by mixing oil, thinner and spar varnish in equal proportions. Here again, I worry about the creation of a total water barrier and the risk of locking in moisture.

Native sealing methods

A traditional finish, used by some native peoples of North America in the past, was a mixture of pine resin and turpentine. There are also reports of melted animal fats and shellac being used.

Recommendations

My favorite finish for hardwood paddles is a 1:1 mixture of linseed and tung oils. I can't think of a good reason for varnishing a one-piece hardwood paddle. However, I do recommend varnish for softwood paddles and epoxy-laminated paddles made from woods with significantly different expansions because of the absolute need to keep water out.

Looking Good: Decorating your paddle

Although at one level, it seems a bit unnecessary to obscure the natural beauty of wood by painting or carving, canoeists have long decorated their paddles and continue to enjoy doing so.

I have been told that paddle art is something of a Canadian characteristic—certainly I have never seen a painted paddle in the United Kingdom. It seems usual to do the painting, or line drawing, on top of a sealing coat of varnish—to prevent the pigment from being absorbed—then to protect the artwork with at least another two coats. If you want to try to re-create native-style designs, you can find plenty of painted paddles in museums, and many

have been depicted in geographic magazines and travel brochures.

Paddles can also be decorated by chip carving, inlay, marquetry and pyrography, and many good books have information on these subjects. It goes without saying that you should practice on scraps of wood until you are proficient.

Even if you don't want to put a painting on your paddle, it is nice to have some sort of personal signature—or a logo if you make paddles professionally. It was not unusual for native paddles to bear the personal mark of the owner. Club paddlers may like to add their club insignia. For this, you can use transfers, rubber stamps and branding. All require the help of specialists, and the first two are suitable only for varnished paddles because they require a protective coating.

The only technique I have had much personal experience with is branding. I had a specialist in an engineering company make a steel brand from artwork I had supplied on a computer disk. The job didn't cost anything—I made him a paddle for his trouble. The only trick was that the design on the brand had

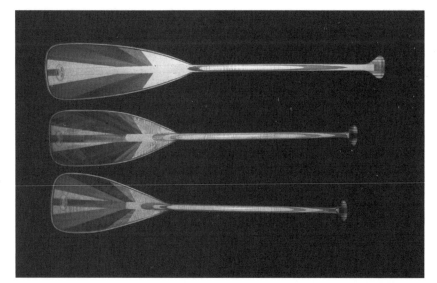

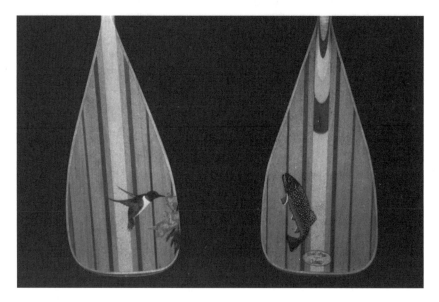

Top: A skillful use of contrasting woods,
top: laminated paddles by Philip Greene,
Wood Song Canoes. Above: Paintings
by Rob Filos on Wood Song paddles.
Photos courtesy Philip Green

to be the mirror image of what I wanted on the paddle. The brand is heated up on a steel plate stood on a gas ring until it is approximately 350 degrees F; the point at which the brand is ready is easily judged by its ability to burn the design on off-cuts of the same wood as the paddle. The brand should not be heated directly on a flame, because this will eventually degrade the design.

It is quite daunting burning into your new paddle, but at least if it goes wrong, it is possible to sand the design off and try again. Care should be taken with laminated paddles made from different woods, because these can burn at different rates. The area to be stamped has to be perfectly flat. I achieve this by pencil shading over the required area, then sanding with sandpaper on a flat block until all the pencil disappears.

With a little imagination, professional-looking designs can be built up from simple shapes by branding with common workshop items such as metal rod (to give circles), the square heads of bolts, hexagonal (Allen) keys and triangular files.

Top left: A collection of authentically decorated paddles by Doug Andrews/photos courtesy Doug Andrews. Above: Paddle with simple marquetry maple leaf. Left: Branding is an effective way of adding a logo.

Care and Repair:
Welcome to the real world

CARE

Having spent considerable time and effort making your paddles, you are likely to take a near parental interest in their well-being, so looking after them will come naturally.

Store your paddles hanging (preferably) or flat so that they do not become bowed by leaning up against a wall. If you do lay your paddles flat, make sure that they are safely out of the way, where someone is not likely to tread on them. When you pull in during a trip for a rest or to camp, don't let your paddles stand in the direct sun, because this might induce warping, especially if they are made of hardwood. It is also important to keep the tip of your paddle blade well sealed. I take a small can of linseed oil with me that I use for touching up, which I do frequently. You can use cooking oil or margarine in a pinch.

Much, if not most, damage to a paddle is incurred during transport, before your canoe even touches the water. Paddles are of an awkward shape to store, and somehow, blades always seem to knock together as you bump along the road in the car. One solution is to make or buy a paddle bag.

Twelve-ounce canvas is a suitable material, because it is very resistant to abrasion and gives a degree of cushioning. Popular models have a divider so that they can take a pair of paddles and are closed by snaps or a drawstring.

The two regions of your paddle that are especially likely to suffer damage are the blade tip and the spot where the shaft meets the gunwale. The extent of gunwale abrasion depends on your personal style of paddling, chiefly how much prying off the canoe you actually do. It used to be fashionable to make a leather collar to fit around the shaft at this point to provide some protection. (A method for doing this is given in *Making Canoe Paddles in Wood*.)

Paddles intended for hard use can be tipped with resin or sheet metal. Adding a protective resin tip to a blade is a rather specialized job that is covered in my book *Advanced Paddlemaking*. However, it is easy to make a simple reinforced blade tip at the same time as you are inserting a spline. Proceed as with the standard splining process, but cut the spline to a line about ⅛ inch inside the end profile of the paddle. With the paddle clamped

vertically (blade uppermost), insert the spline, then fill the recessed edge with a mixture of epoxy or phenol-resorcinol resin glue and powdered silica, in the proportion 5 milliliters resin to 10 grams silica. This forms a mix that is stiff enough not to run out of the end of the blade. Cover the two ends of the slot with masking tape to keep the resin in place. Tidy up with sandpaper when the resin has set.

Many canoeists carry a spare "all-terrain" paddle that they can pull out when rocks appear, and so they are able to spare their finer paddles. In any case, try as much as possible to avoid pushing off rocks or the bottom with your paddle.

REPAIR

Shaft repair
There are two main options for repairing a broken shaft, depending upon how close to the blade the break has occurred. If the break is about 6 inches or more above the throat, then it can be repaired directly. If it is closer to the top of the blade, then it is probably a relaminating job. I have only ever done these jobs using my bandsaw. While it may be possible to use

hand tools, I have no direct experience with this.

To do a direct shaft repair, the paddle has to be pushed back together so that it is more or less as it was before the accident. Take special care to ensure that the shaft is perfectly aligned across the break and that the blade and grip are in the same plane. The shaft is now splinted using a batten and strong tape to hold it in line while the first part of the repair is done. Carefully cut a shallow arc at least 8 inches long, extending into about the center of the shaft. The cut should be as smooth as possible and can be cleaned up with sandpaper on a foam block. The next step is to glue in a series of thin laminations that you can clamp in to conform to the cut that you have just made, as shown at right. Have a sheet of plastic under the joint to prevent glue from sticking to your work surface.

With one side of the shaft replaced by new wood, you now have to repeat the operation on the other side of the break. This is a little easier because the newly added laminations form

Repairing a broken shaft

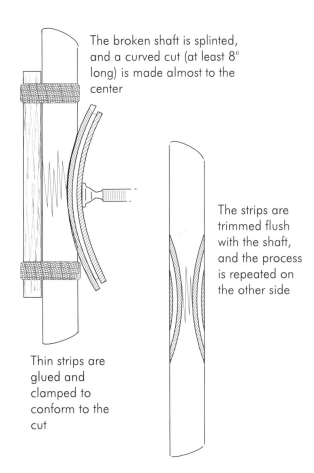

The broken shaft is splinted, and a curved cut (at least 8" long) is made almost to the center

The strips are trimmed flush with the shaft, and the process is repeated on the other side

Thin strips are glued and clamped to conform to the cut

Making a resin tip

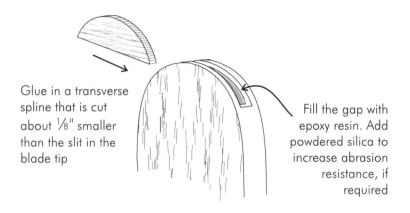

Glue in a transverse spline that is cut about $1/8$" smaller than the slit in the blade tip

Fill the gap with epoxy resin. Add powdered silica to increase abrasion resistance, if required

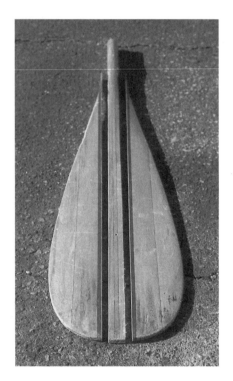

The blade "wings" have been cut off this paddle with a broken shaft, above. The laminations of darker wood make convenient lines to follow with the saw. Note how water has seeped up under the varnish at the tip. This paddle has definitely been neglected.

a splint for the joint. The repair will look best if the second cut is as near a mirror image as possible to the first one.

With both sides of the break made good, it remains to blend the excess wood back into the shaft with a block plane. Finally, give the repair a good sanding, and refinish to match the rest of the paddle. You cannot really hide this type of repair, so the next best thing is to use contrasting woods to turn the repair into a feature.

Relaminating

This is a job for enthusiasts only. It is hard to justify the time and effort (although it is significantly quicker than making a new paddle) unless the paddle was a revered family heirloom. The idea here is to cut along the blade, following the line of the shaft, to liberate the two blade "wings." The cut edges of these are then trued up and glued back onto a new shaft. That's the theory anyway.

If the paddle is of laminated construction, then the joints between laminations make excellent reference lines for cutting, especially if a dark glue was used. If the paddle is (or, rather, was) a one-piece, then you will need to draw guidelines along the blade in line with the edges of the shaft. Cut a shade outside the lines to allow for truing up. Even with very little practice, it is quite easy to cut to a line by eye on a bandsaw. It is essential that your cuts are perpendicular to the plane of the blade. Because the blade is cambered, it will not sit quietly on the bandsaw table. To make a stable platform for the blade and to hold it perpendicular to the saw blade, screw the shaft to a scrap of timber and shim out the edges of the blade until it is horizontal. Don't worry about the screw holes in the shaft; this is to be discarded. With the paddle now held firm and level, it is a much simpler job to cut along the edge of the shaft.

To true up the cut, use a piece of 60-grit paper on a 10-inch square-sided sanding block. This length of sanding block should ensure that the edges finish up perfectly straight. This sanding step demands a little patience but is not difficult. Because the edges of the paddle wings are curved, you need to be a little creative to be able to clamp them onto the new shaft while the glue dries. Trace out the curve of the blade onto a couple of pieces of scrap wood, then cut out. These scrap pieces are now a complementary shape to the blade and are used to clamp the whole setup into position. This is clearly shown in the photo on page 119. Support the blade wings centrally on the shaft with panel pins in exactly the same way as described for laminating a new paddle.

After the glue has set, it is an easy job to trim the shaft down to the line of the blade. The shaft and new grip are finished off in the usual way. Alternatively, you might want to graft on the original grip to the new shaft.

The refurbished paddle should be as strong, or stronger, than the original.

Repairing a split or chipped blade

Splits not only arise from impacts but can also grow from tiny drying-out (hydrocycling) cracks that form because the blade tip has not been kept adequately sealed. Once such a split has started, it is difficult to contain; it tends to let in even more water, thereby amplifying the problem. Edge grain in the blade is more susceptible to impact cracks than is flat grain but less susceptible to drying-out cracks.

It is sometimes possible to cut the split out and replace with a fillet of new wood. A relatively easy way to do this for a narrow split is to run the blade onto the table saw, using the saw fence to keep the cut straight. With a fillet of wood glued into the slot, the split should be well and truly stopped.

If you see hydrocycling cracks beginning to form, perhaps the best course of action is to spline the tip of the blade, as already described.

Minor chips out of the blade edge are best fixed using a glue/sawdust filler. Woodworking books tell you that a repair done using filler made from sawdust from the same type of wood will be invisible. Invisible is not the

word that I would choose. Even transparent epoxy glue darkens the sawdust color appreciably. However, with a little trial and error and a range of woods at your disposal, it should be possible to come up with a reasonably good match. The sawdust has to be very fine — the stuff out of the dust bag

After truing up the cuts with a long sanding block, the blade wings are glued onto a new shaft. The thin blade strips were supported on panel pins taped into the shaft, shown after gluing, top. Above: Clamp the blade with scraps cut to match the blade outline.

The first time on the water with a paddle you've built yourself is an exciting moment. Above, testing a double-blade paddle.

on a belt sander is ideal. You can also quickly make the tiny amounts of sawdust required with 60-grit paper, and doing the job by hand makes it easier to blend the dusts from different woods to get the color that you want.

Major damage to the blade is probably best tackled by planing off the broken section, gluing on a new piece and shaping to match. It may be possible to trace the undamaged side of the paddle to get an outline to work to.

PERFORMANCE CHARACTERISTICS

Things to look out for when test-driving your paddle

The moment you head out on the water with a new paddle is one that is eagerly anticipated. All the theoretical speculations on paddle design don't amount to much when compared with finding out just how the paddle performs in real life. If you are new to paddling, however, it may take a while to appreciate the more subtle aspects of the paddle's performance. Here are some "test drive" suggestions to help you evaluate the quality of your new paddle. Many of these factors are easier to appreciate if you take along some other paddles for comparison. Paddles frequently show their own idiosyncrasies, such as a particular pattern of vor-

texing, a little whip of the blade at the end of a stroke or a characteristic sound when slicing. Tuning into these peculiarities adds charm to creating and using your own unique paddles.

If you decide to modify your paddle in light of these tests, you will be at a great advantage if you have chosen an oil finish—you simply have to wipe oil over the bare wood exposed during modification.

Veering test. Slice the paddle sideways in the water between strokes. A good paddle will slice without undue resistance and will travel in a straight line, without veering to one side. If the paddle does veer, it means that the camber on the two blade faces is not symmetrical. Check this by eye by laying a straightedge across the faces of the blade. You should be able to remedy this problem by some additional carving. If the paddle does not veer but still does not slice easily or it is noisy, the edges/shoulders are probably too thick.

Flutter test. Pull the blade hard, with the power face perpendicular to your canoe. The paddle should feel absolutely stable and should not "flutter," that is, wobble from side to side. Flutter is caused by the blade (or spine) being asymmetrical or by inefficient damping because the paddle is too stiff.

Noise on entry. Close your eyes and concentrate on the noise ("song") of the paddle as you move along. If the paddle is noisy, you could try thinning down the tip a little.

Slip point. With your canoe tied up, make strokes of increasing power until the paddle begins to "misfire" appreciably. This is the slip point, the point at which water is no longer held efficiently by the blade. Although this is a very subjective test, it does give you a feel for how efficient the paddle is for power strokes. It does not give an absolute rating but does allow you to rank a series of paddles in order, so it is useful to have at least one other paddle along as a reference.

Steering moment. Stop your canoe and perform a sweep stroke—stick your paddle out at right angles, and pull back and into the canoe sharply. See how far you turn.

Maximum comfortable stroke rate. Experiment with the stroke rate that you can comfortably maintain for a fixed time, say two minutes.

Water shedding. Watch the water coming off the blade between strokes as you go. Try to rate this alongside your reference paddles.

More rapid water runoff means a lighter paddle.

Flip. Try to become aware of the flip in the blade at the end of the power phase of each stroke. If this is very pronounced, the blade is probably too flexible and you are losing efficiency.

Balance in use. Immerse the paddle, then lift out quickly and find the balance point. Ideally, this should be just below your lower grip region.

Test-driving a new voyageur paddle (in bow) and a new Sugar Island paddle (in stern).

Origins:
Paddlemaking in the native tradition

Text and photos © David Gidmark

While a paddle is a simple and elegant implement, it doesn't have to be humdrum. Yet throughout North America, when you see a paddle in use or watch one being made, it is inevitably of the beavertail design. A lithe and attractive paddle in itself, it seems somehow to crowd out the other beautiful North American Indian paddles. Much is lost through such homogenization.

It is encouraging to note how accessible paddlemaking is—or should be. A parent and a child as young as 12 can work on paddles together. The main tools needed in making a paddle—an ax and a crooked knife—are also relatively accessible. A craftsperson of reasonable skill, though new to making a paddle, can purchase a crooked knife and board for a paddle for $20 on a Saturday morning and have a finished paddle by evening. As the reader will soon discover, there is no need for hun-

dreds of dollars' worth of sanders, bandsaws and other mechanical equipment to make a paddle. Such workshop overkill betrays the simplicity of the North American Indian lifestyle. It is analogous to cutting a pizza with a laser.

Although the paddle is one of the easiest things to make in woodworking, it is no less rewarding for that. It is especially satisfying to make a paddle from a standing tree. Wood comes from the forest, after all, before it comes from the lumberyard. Harvesting the material directly from nature helps us to view this process as the North American Indians saw it. And the paddles of the various North American Indian tribes in this book will allow the reader to create his or her own collection of the various tribal types.

The Algonquin are often referred to in discussing paddlemaking in this chapter, but most of the techniques are common to

many other tribes. A few paddles from outside North America are included. When one looks at paddles from around the world, one is struck anew by the particular variety and beauty of the North American Indian paddles.

Because the crooked knife is the most important tool in making a paddle—the crooked knife is a tool the reader will come to cherish—and because it is sometimes hard to find and descriptions of making one are scarce, I have included here a section on making a crooked knife. For casting an experienced eye on that part of this chapter, I owe thanks to Douglas Brown of Wyoming. The photos of making a crooked knife were taken with the help of David Fleming of Ontario, who knows much more about the process than I do. David also provided extremely useful input into the paddle section, particularly with respect to the qualities of the different woods.

PADDLE WOODS

Most woods can be used for making paddles. Qualities you should seek are strength, beauty, lightness, flexibility and ease of carving. No wood has all these qualities—perhaps ash comes closest—but with

luck, you'll find one that will have two or more of these characteristics. You'll want to make paddles out of various woods to get the experience of working with different kinds of woods with the crooked

knife. Generally, however, dry wood is harder to work with a crooked knife than green wood is.

White birch is an acceptable wood for paddles and was used often by the Algonquin. It is easy to carve when green but prone to warp. It doesn't split out as well as maple, but—unlike maple—it makes a good, light paddle. Yellow birch is not recommended, because it is difficult to work; the grain reverses, and it is hard to work with a crooked knife. Sugar, or rock, maple makes a superior paddle and was perhaps the most common wood used by the Algonquin for paddlemaking. It works well when green but is difficult to work when seasoned. Maple splits well and gives a smooth finish that feels nice in the hand. It is a bit heavy, so the blade should be thin. Master canoe builder Jerry Stelmok favors maple for paddles. Cherry is an attractive wood that is relatively easy to carve when green but terribly difficult when dry. On a canoe trip, it can prove to be not as strong as you would like. It can be weak under tension and can snap easily. It is expensive to buy at a lumber store, and a good piece can likewise be hard to locate in the woods.

Because of its flexibility and strength, ash is the first choice for a paddle, especially for use in a wilderness canoe trip. Although somewhat hard to work, it is worth the effort.

Three satisfactory woods when

you are learning how to make a paddle are butternut, poplar and basswood, because they are softer and easier to carve and their grain is not tricky. Poplar and basswood are inexpensive to buy as well.

Spruce makes a splendid light and springy paddle and is easy to carve, even when dry, but it is hard to find a knot-free length. White cedar is fine for a learner—though not as strong as spruce—and makes a light and effective child's paddle. You can also use a white

Basil Dewache, Kitigan Zibi Algonquin, with an ash paddle he made using a crooked knife.

Above left to right: If you buy your lumber commercially, search for a board relatively free of knot holes and trace the paddle's shape on it. When harvesting your own wood, split the log using an ax and a wooden mallet. A wooden wedge helps to split the half log farther along its length.

cedar paddle on a lake or when you know that you are not going to put great pressure on it. A sleek, light cedar paddle is quite elegant when used in a birchbark canoe.

Western red cedar has many of the same characteristics and uses as white cedar; however, it is more brittle than the latter. Of the woods used in western North America for paddles, Sitka spruce and western yellow cedar are suitable for pad-

dles. Pacific yew is tough, very springy and takes a good polish.

Woods that aren't recommended are oaks, because they are hard to carve; elm and beech, because they warp severely; hemlock and tamarack, because they are knotty and splinter easily; balsam, because it breaks; and walnut and mahogany, because they are not necessary — they are for show-offs.

MAKING A PADDLE

You can obtain wood for making a paddle in two ways: one is to buy wood from a lumberyard, and the other is to cut a log in the woods. Both have advantages and disadvantages. The best thing about a lumberyard is that it is generally accessible. You could theoretically buy an ax and a crooked knife in the morning, go to the lumberyard for a board and finish your paddle by the end of the day. In comparison with what you must sometimes pay for a finished paddle, a board

out of which you can carve a paddle doesn't cost much. The great disadvantage of buying a board, however, is that it will be dried and therefore significantly harder to carve with a crooked knife.

When you are buying your board, whether hardwood or softwood, take along an existing paddle to gauge the board for clear wood. Trace the form of the paddle onto the board. It is useful to do this before you leave the lumberyard to make sure you won't have any knots in the finished paddle. Good spruce and cedar boards often have knots, but you can eventually find a board that is clear enough to trace a paddle shape around a few knots. Most lumberyards will allow you to pick through lumber in search of the right piece.

Be sure you have the dimensions of the finished paddle in mind before you leave the lumberyard. Boards are often 1 inch thick, but since most paddles have shafts that are also 1 inch thick, a 1-inch board won't allow you to take off any wood. Some paddles have shafts $1\frac{1}{8}$ inches thick—even more reason to be careful when selecting a board.

When you cut the paddle out of the board, allow a good $\frac{1}{4}$ inch to be taken off with the crooked knife from all dimensions of the paddle. That way, you'll avoid making your paddle too thin or too narrow.

Harvesting your paddle wood yourself in the woods tends to be a more rewarding experience than buying a board in a lumber-yard. It is not without its travails, though.

Wood does come from nature, after all, and you will be able to get a much better feel for the wood by cutting the tree yourself. Cutting paddle wood in the forest also helps to train the eye to pick out trees of various species and quality. You might go in the woods to pick out an ash tree with a clear 5 feet on the trunk. But once there, you can't help but notice whether the birch trees and the spruce trees in the ash grove also have clear lengths on their trunks. The eye must be trained to see. You'll come

away with a much better appreciation of what nature has to offer and just how difficult it is to locate quality materials.

If you plan to harvest from private land, you'll need to get permission from the owner beforehand. If the trees you're looking at are growing on public land, go to the public authority. You may require a special permit. On public land, logging companies often have timber rights, so you may have to check with a lumber company.

You might have to locate a tree 10 or more inches in diameter. The log you cut from the tree will have to be clear of knots, or at the very least, the area from which the paddle will emerge will have to be clear of knots.

This is much more difficult to find in some species than in others. A large white birch tree, for example, will usually yield a straight 5-foot log that is knot-free at least in one of the quarter logs. Spruce is something else again. Even though you have many large spruce trees in an area, it could take you a long time to find a straight, clear section of a tree from which to cut your paddle.

When you have found a suitable tree, cut it down, avoiding the flare at the bottom of the trunk. Then cut a log slightly longer than the length of your paddle.

Split the log in half from the top end to the butt end. You can use two axes, but be sure not to hit steel against steel. Hitting one ax head against another could endanger your eyes and also cause the ax heads to break. Instead, hit the ax head with a wooden mallet.

First, score a line about $\frac{1}{4}$ inch deep on the top end of the log.

Man's spruce paddle

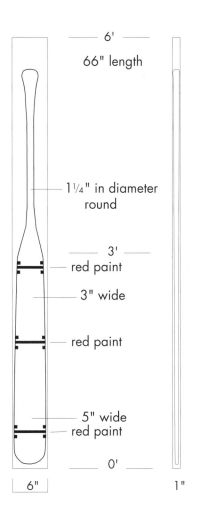

Adapted from Canoe Construction in a Cree Cultural Tradition *by J. Garth Taylor (Ottawa: National Museums of Canada, 1980).*

When taking off wood with an ax, avoid overtiring your arm by not holding the ax too far from the ax head, top. Instead, grip the ax close to the head, above. This will also allow for better workmanship.

That way, the split will begin at that line when the log starts to cleave. Use the other ax, or a wooden wedge, to continue the split down the log. If you happen to have found a crooked log, you'll quickly see the advantage of a straight-grain log. Don't settle for less than perfect materials, or it could take you days—rather than hours—to make your paddle with an ax and a crooked knife.

While still in the woods, split the half log in half again. Quarter logs are easier to carry out.

For your first paddle, select the best of the four quarter logs. The quarter log should be straight and knot-free. The paddle blank will be about 6 inches wide and 1¼ inches thick, and you need to make sure before you leave the woods that the blank is in the quarter log somewhere.

A freshly cut log is somewhat more favorable than is a kiln-dried board, because green wood is much easier to carve. Remember that you can negate this advantage if you've settled for a quarter log with many knots in it. It is critical to have a sharp ax and crooked knife. With clear wood and sharp tools, you'll save much time.

Before beginning to use the ax, you should split off as much wood as possible. It is easier to take off wood by splitting than by using an ax. And it is easier again to take off wood with an ax than it is with a crooked knife.

To shape the blank, put the quarter log on a block of wood and start chopping. Although many people use an ax, not many use an ax in actual woodworking. Hold the ax next to the head—not down on the handle—

so that your arm does not tire too easily.

At first, you may want to keep your paddle model next to your work site so that you can use it as a guide. When you get used to the shapes and the tools, you'll be able to work without a model.

Skilled axmen (I'm thinking now especially of the old Indian birchbark canoe builders such as César Newashish) are able to carve a virtually finished paddle with a sharp ax.

When you've taken the paddle down about as much as you can with the ax, it is time to finish the job with the crooked knife.

You should sit comfortably as you are working with a crooked knife. The best way is to sit on a chopping block with your legs at ease in front of you. Northern Cree craftsmen usually sat on the ground with their legs folded back under them, but this position is uncomfortable for most people.

As you carve your paddle with the crooked knife, you'll want to rest the distant end of the paddle on your left thigh or on the ground. Don't hold the paddle in the air as you are carving; this offers little support for the carving stroke and is a bad work habit in general.

It is important to remember how to place the paddle as you are carving. If your left hand is holding the paddle on the shaft and you're carving on the blade, for example, make sure that the blade comes past your body on your right side, assuming you are right-handed. Do not point the paddle toward your stomach, because the end of the knife stroke could cut your shirt—or your skin. Some people have strange-looking belly buttons; this is not the best way to alter them.

Pull the crooked knife toward you. Hold it palm up, with your thumb braced against the end of the handle; if you don't, you'll need a much stronger grip and your hand will tire that much faster.

Holding the handle of the crooked knife so that your hand is fairly close to the blade—not out on the handle—minimizes the strength required. Conserving strength is important if you have a lot of work to do with the crooked knife.

You should also conserve strength by cutting the wood on the crooked knife blade near to the handle. This won't always be possible, because on occasion, the only way you'll be able to work the wood (on the blade of the paddle, for instance) is by working the wood across the blade. Then you'll be carving close to the far (curved) end of the blade, which requires more strength. Turning the paddle end for end to deal with tricky grain might also require carving near the end of the blade.

Begin slowly to learn to use a crooked knife. Once you get used to this indispensable tool, you'll swear by it. Cut off only a little wood at a time so that you can be more accurate initially. Later, you'll be able to go faster.

If you're right-handed, hold the paddle with your left hand while you carve. Never hold the paddle with your left hand below the stroke; in other words, don't cut toward your left hand. Always place your left hand above the stroke. You've probably been taught not to cut toward yourself

Above: In descending order, a hoof knife (a factory-manufactured knife used in canoe building) with the end of the handle sawed off to accommodate the thumb; an unaltered hoof knife; a Cree-made crooked knife, with an old file for a blade and the end of an old ax handle serving as the knife handle; and a hoof knife with a plastic handle, very usable and affordable at about four dollars. Left: Hold the paddle with the left hand. The knife should be drawn away from the left hand and past the right side of the body. Below: The right way to hold a crooked knife—the hand is close to the blade, and the thumb placed along the end of the knife, not over it.

Bird's eye maple paddle

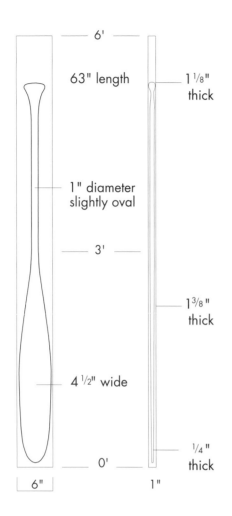

6'

63" length

1 1/8" thick

1" diameter slightly oval

3'

1 3/8" thick

4 1/2" wide

1/4" thick

0'

6"

1"

Maple paddle

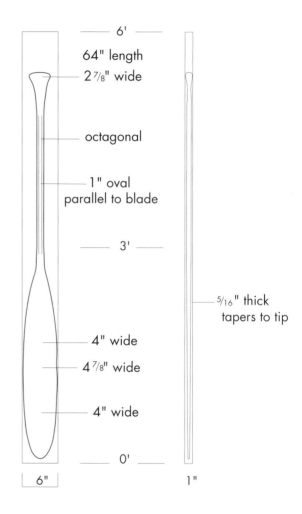

6'

64" length

2 7/8" wide

octagonal

1" oval parallel to blade

3'

5/16" thick tapers to tip

4" wide

4 7/8" wide

4" wide

0'

6"

1"

with a knife, but once you learn (carefully!) how to use a crooked knife, you'll find it an extremely useful implement. As you become more adept with a crooked knife, you'll be able to put a finish on the paddle that is without knife marks, which is a sure sign of a skilled craftsperson.

As you progress, it will become necessary to turn the paddle end for end a number of times to accommodate the contours of the paddle (where the handle meets the shaft and where the blade meets the shaft, for example) and also to deal with the vicissitudes of the grain. It would be wonderful if the grain were as straight as the finished paddle is supposed to be, but it doesn't work that way in real life.

In the case I'm describing, remember, the paddle is being carved from green wood, and to avoid excessive twist in the finished paddle, you must do your best to dry the wood. The Algonquin way to do this is to leave excess wood (maybe 1/8 to 1/4 inch) all around the paddle. Then put a nail in the handle end of the paddle, tie a cord to the nail, and hang the paddle in a tree for a couple of weeks. The paddle may twist as the wood dries. If it does, you can carve the twist out of the paddle after a few weeks by taking off excess wood in the logical places.

Your paddle is now nearly finished. If your strokes with the crooked knife have not been as sleek as you'd like them in the beginning, you might want to use sandpaper to smooth the paddle.

You can finish the paddle with a few coats of varnish, sanding lightly between coats.

If the tip of your paddle eventually becomes frayed in use, you can restore it by carving the tip smooth with your crooked knife.

And don't forget, now that you're adept with an ax and a crooked knife, you'll be able to make a paddle in the woods if you happen to break one on a canoe trip.

THE CROOKED KNIFE

There are a couple of things that are quite striking about the crooked knife (*mokotâgan*, in Algonquin) within the contemporary context: the first is its great utility; the second is the fact that it is seldom seen today, although scores of Indian tribes used them in the past. It is thought that the prehistoric crooked knife blade may in fact have been the incisor tooth of the beaver.

Some time ago in Quebec, a memoir of wilderness life in the north in the early part of the 20th century appeared. The title itself— *Ma femme, mon hache et mon couteau croche* (*My Wife, My Axe and My Crooked Knife*)—points toward the importance of this tool in boreal culture.

The craftsman follows a simple progression in taking down wood for paddles, snowshoes or birchbark canoes. As much wood as possible is taken off in splitting the tree, then with the ax and lastly with the crooked knife. Although a drawknife takes off more wood more quickly than a crooked knife does, you will achieve finer, more precise work with a crooked knife than you will with a drawknife.

The classic image of the Indian craftsman is a man sitting on the ground or on a wood block, deftly and smoothly drawing the crooked knife toward him scores of times until he has fashioned his paddle or a rib for a birchbark canoe. It is hard to think of a more useful tool or of a tool with which the craftsman is likely to develop a more intimate relationship.

Making a crooked knife

It is easy to make a crooked knife using a worn-out file. A 1/2-inch file doesn't require as much shaping or filing as does a bigger file. A Nicholson file ($3 to $4 new) has a high carbon content and is one of the best. Globe files are also suitable. For blade stock, you can also cut an old crosscut saw blade to give the approximate shape of a file.

The steel must first be annealed, or softened. Use a woodstove or a barbecue with coals to make your fire. In the woodstove, the fire should be made with small- to medium-size pieces of hardwood. For a hot fire, keep the draft on the stove open.

To maximize the heat, put the file in the fire when the fire is half-burned down to coals. Use gloves

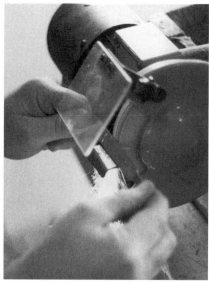

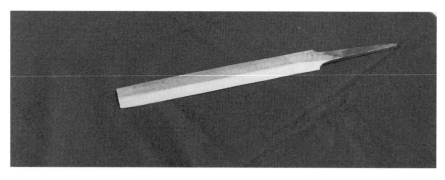

Top left and right: Using a wet water wheel, grind the teeth from the file. Above: A bevel needs to be ground on the top side of the file, as seen here.

and pliers to hold the tang of the file.

The steel will start to heat in three to four minutes. You should heat the steel until it becomes bright cherry red, about 1,450 degrees F. If it is dull red only, it's too cool; if it goes to dull orange, it is too hot. Look at the color in semi-darkness so that you can see it properly.

When the file has been heated to a bright cherry red, remove it from the fire and put it in the ashes or in a coffee can full of sand overnight to cool.

Next morning, file it with a new file to see whether the steel has been properly annealed. Then the teeth must be ground from the file. This can be done with a fresh file, a wet water wheel or a grinding

wheel. If the grinding wheel is dry, the file must be dipped in cold water frequently.

A bevel about $1/4$ inch wide is now made on the top side of the file. The teeth on the bottom of the file must be taken off for easier carving. The bottom should be as polished as the bevel.

Effective with softwood, a shallow bevel takes off a lot of wood quickly but can also dig into grain easily. A steep bevel is good for hardwoods and fine trimming — getting out the knife marks on cedar ribs in a birchbark canoe, for example.

A shallow bevel gives flat wood shavings, while a steep bevel gives curled shavings. It's useful to have two knives, one with a steep-beveled blade for snowshoes and hardwood paddles, another with a shallow-beveled blade for birch-bark canoes (cedar) and softwood paddles.

A hook about $3/16$ inch long must be put on the end of the tang to hold the file in the wooden handle. Heat the end of the tang to a dull cherry-red color with a propane torch, and then bend it with pliers.

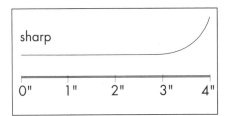

sharp

0"　1"　2"　3"　4"

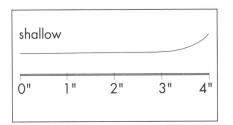

shallow

0"　1"　2"　3"　4"

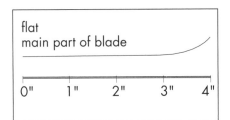

flat
main part of blade

0"　1"　2"　3"　4"

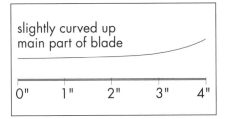

slightly curved up
main part of blade

0"　1"　2"　3"　4"

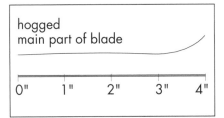

hogged
main part of blade

0"　1"　2"　3"　4"

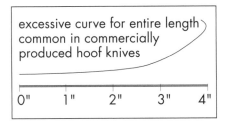

excessive curve for entire length
common in commercially
produced hoof knives

0"　1"　2"　3"　4"

Left: Illustrations of possible curves for the crooked knife blade. Top and above: How to put a short hook on the end of the tang and how to bend the end of the blade to its proper curvature.

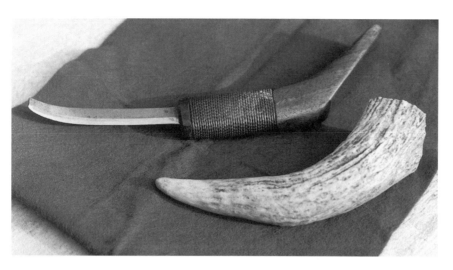

The handle of a crooked knife is sometimes made from antler.

Bending the tip of the tang first helps to determine whether the file is too brittle.

In the next step, create the curve at the end of the blade by heating the tip with a propane torch until it is once more a dull cherry red and then bending it with pliers. The degree of curve is a matter of taste and usage. The curve can be either shallow or steep.

A shallow curve allows you to work on the far side of a wide piece of wood. A sharp curve has a tendency to gauge when you are working with it on the far side of the piece, but it is good for carving items such as bowls and spoons.

A good curve on the end of the blade can also be made by pounding the cherry-red end around a pipe 1 inch in diameter.

As for the main part of the blade itself, you want to achieve only a suspicion of a curve in the last half of the blade.

Although you certainly want to avoid a hogged blade, even a flat blade can dig into the wood too much.

Hardening the blade

To harden the blade, heat it to bright cherry red, and then quench it in a can of engine oil. Do not quench it in water. Do not harden the tang, because that would make it brittle.

After hardening and quenching the blade, get a good file and test the blade. The blade should at this stage be too hard to cut. You can now sand the blade both to make it look good and to take away the blackness and scale to see when it takes on the proper color during tempering. The blade is sharpened with a flat file by pushing off the bevel, and then the blade is touched up with a whetstone.

Tempering

To temper (soften) the steel, heat an oven to 450 degrees F and put the blade in for a few minutes until it turns a dark straw (bronze) color. Then polish and sharpen the blade.

---

top bevel about ¼ inch wide

extremely slight sharpening
on bottom of bevel,
leaving it close to flat

Sharpen the bevel and also sharpen an extremely slight angle on the bottom of the blade, while still leaving it close to flat.

As the knife gets more use, it becomes polished on the bottom and cuts more easily.

Making the handle

The handle for your crooked knife can be made out of cherry, walnut, birch or most other hardwoods. It should not be made out of a dense, coarse-grained hard-to-work wood like oak. Nor should it be made out of a softwood, as the wood would eventually loosen up in use and the blade would have too much play. As well, crooked knife handles are sometimes made of antler.

Trace the handle on a block of wood, and then cut it out. The handle ultimately should be made to fit the palm comfortably, incorporating a recessed place for the thumb. Use a spokeshave or a wood rasp to round off the edges on the wood handle. As you work, occasionally fit the handle in your palm to make sure it feels comfortable.

The shape of the tang should then be carefully traced on the top side of the handle. Trace closely so that the blade is not loose when in use. The best placing of the blade is halfway from top to bottom — neither high nor low on the handle.

The place for the tang is made by first chain-drilling through the tracing. The area is then chiseled out. Take extra care so that the tang will fit snugly. The hook at the end of the tang fits down $1/8$ inch or a little more at the end of the chiseled-out area. Then carve a slip of hardwood to fit precisely in the hollowed-out area above the tang. Carve the slip, and then shave it (so as not to cut too much) as it gets closer to a perfect fit.

Make a recess (about $1/8$ inch deep and 2 inches wide) around the handle to accept the wrapping that holds the slip in place. Wrap this hollow with cod line (also called heavy ice-fishing line), which is usually green cotton about $1/8$ inch in diameter ($1/8$-inch nylon cord can also be used). Pull the line tightly around the handle in the recess, and then finish through a loop, which you then pull under the wrapping.

You can give an attractive finish to the knife handle by rubbing in a few drops of linseed oil or gun oil.

A note about blacksmiths: They are fine, competent people, but most have not used a crooked knife. In other words, your blacksmith may make a crooked knife for you that is unusable, if only because the best sense of how to make the tool comes from having used it extensively.

This means that you'll probably have to make your own crooked knife, or — if you ask a blacksmith to make one for you — you will have to have used one extensively in order to give him the proper instructions. Then see that he follows them meticulously.

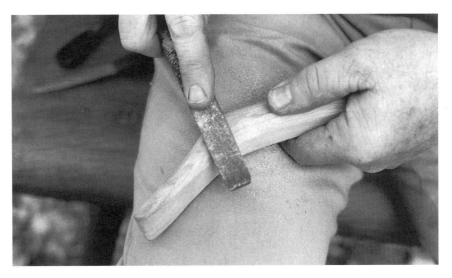

Trace the shape of the knife handle on a block of wood, top, and use a wood rasp to round off the handle's edges, above.

The shape of the tang is carefully traced on the top side of the handle, right, then the notch for the tang is first chain-drilled, then chiseled out, center left and right. A slip of hardwood is carved to fit perfectly in the notch for the tang, bottom.

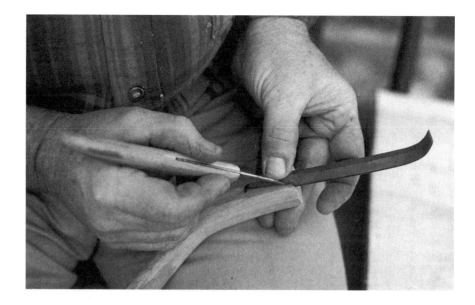

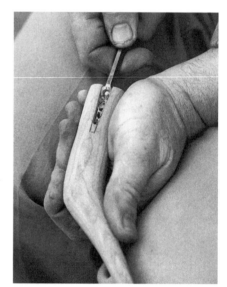

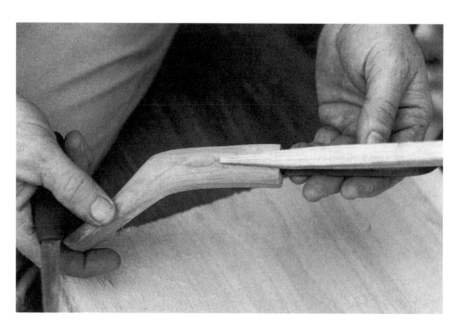

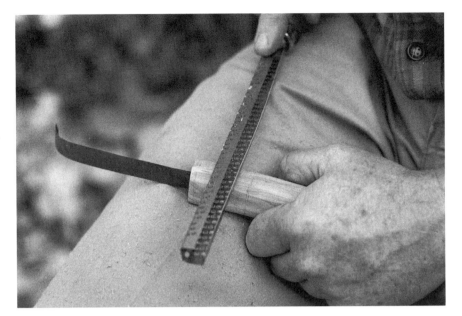

Once you create a recess in the handle to accept the wrapping that holds the slip and tang in place, left, the handle is ready to be wrapped with line, center. With a loop, pull the cod line to hide it, and finish the wrapping of the handle, bottom left. Bottom right: The finished crooked knife in use.

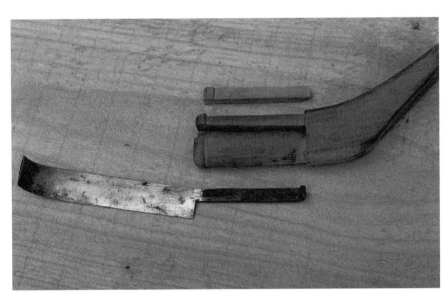

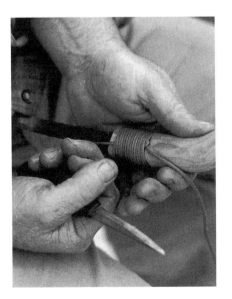

Paddle Plans

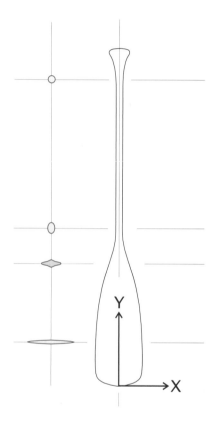

To offer a reasonably wide choice for different water conditions, I've included plans for six standard single-blade paddles. I have also selected a bent-shaft paddle suitable for long-distance touring or racing, a child's paddle and a double-blade design. Each plan includes a table of offsets to allow you to make a pattern for the blade. Information on turning a table of offsets into a blade pattern is given in Chapter 5 (Paddle-making Basics). The dimensions are given in inches and 32nds; for example, $1/19$ means 1 $19/32$ inches.

The dimensions given for shaft and blade thickness are typical figures which should give you a good general-purpose paddle but which you may need to optimize for specific water conditions. Refer to Chapter 2 (Design) for information on fine-tuning the paddle to your specific needs. Because choice of grip is a personal matter, I have included a separate collection of grip plans. Take your choice of these to use on your paddle. All grips are suitable for use with any blade design, with the exception of the asymmetric grip, which is specifically designed for use on a bent-shaft paddle.

The overall length of your paddle should be worked out using one of the methods given in Chapter 2. Remember to work out your required grip span and then add this to the blade length given on the plan.

All designs are © Graham Warren 2000. Written permission is required for commercial production of paddles to these designs.

Generalized shaft plan

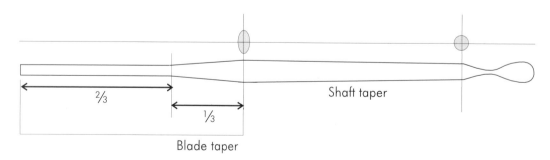

2/3

1/3

Shaft taper

Blade taper

Far left: Northwoods paddles made by Alexander Conover based on a Penobscot design. Blades are decorated using many methods, such as this ink drawing by Garrett Conover, left. Photos by Alexandra Conover

Key paddle dimensions—a quick reference

Shaft cross section (hardwood): $1\frac{1}{8}$" round or
  $1\frac{1}{16}$" by $1\frac{1}{4}$" elliptical   pages 28-29
Shaft cross section (softwood): $1\frac{1}{4}$" round
  or $1\frac{1}{8}$" by $1\frac{3}{8}$" elliptical   pages 28-29
Blade thickness at center: $\frac{1}{4}$" to $\frac{3}{8}$"   pages 37, 97
Blade thickness at edges: $\frac{1}{16}$" to $\frac{3}{32}$"   page 36
Blade length to fit the paddler   pages 29-31

Traditional beavertail

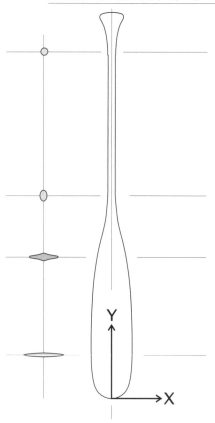

Offsets
Inches/32nds

Y	X
0/16	1/16
1	2/3
2	2/21
4	3/2
6	3/6
8	3/8
10	3/7
12	3/5
14	3/2
16	2/30
18	2/24
20	2/15
22	2/4
24	1/22
26	1/4
28	0/23
30	0/17

Suggested Dimensions

Overall blank thickness: 1 ¼"

Shaft: 1 ¼" x 1 ¹⁄₁₆" at throat to 1 ¹⁄₁₆" x 1 ¹⁄₁₆" at neck

Blade edges: ³⁄₃₂"

Blade thickness: ³⁄₈"

Traditional beavertail

Blade length: 28"
Blade width: 6½"
Surface area: 148 sq.in.

This blade is an elegant classic design that seems to have its origin in native Maliseet and Passamaquoddy paddles. The blade area of 148 square inches makes it a comfortable paddle for short tours, and the broad tip gives reasonable impact resistance. The version I made for this book has a scalloped guide grip and balances perfectly, just above the throat, when dry.

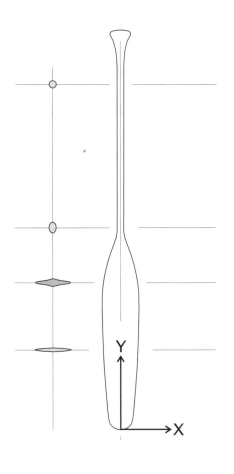

Offsets
Inches/32nds

Y	X
0/16	1/13
1	1/24
2	1/29
4	2/4
6	2/10
8	2/15
10	2/19
12	2/22
14	2/24
16	2/25
18	2/25
20	2/23
22	2/15
24	2/0
26	1/10
27	0/30
28	0/19
29	0/16

Suggested Dimensions

Overall blank thickness: $1\frac{1}{4}$"

Shaft: $1\frac{1}{4}$" x $1\frac{1}{16}$" at throat to $1\frac{1}{16}$" x $1\frac{1}{16}$" at neck

Blade edges: $\frac{3}{32}$"

Blade thickness: $\frac{3}{8}$"

Ottertail
Blade length: 28"
Blade width: $5\frac{5}{8}$"
Surface area: 128 sq.in.

The tapered blade of the ottertail makes it a quiet paddle. The fact that the wide part of the blade is high up the blade means that this design is a little less efficient for steering than the beavertail is. The tip is also more vulnerable. People choose this design for its quietness and ease of handling. A nice deep-water touring paddle. The design is considered good for freestyle paddling; being narrow, it is easier to rotate in the water than are wider designs, thus allowing the fluid linking of strokes.

Voyageur

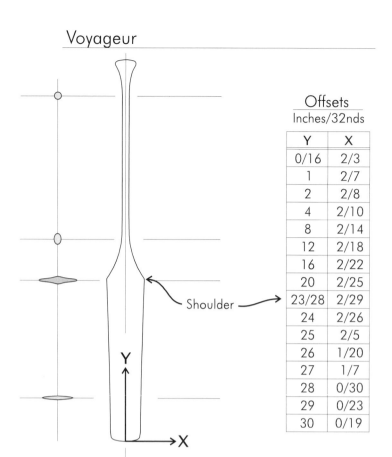

Offsets
Inches/32nds

Y	X
0/16	2/3
1	2/7
2	2/8
4	2/10
8	2/14
12	2/18
16	2/22
20	2/25
23/28	2/29
24	2/26
25	2/5
26	1/20
27	1/7
28	0/30
29	0/23
30	0/19

Shoulder

Suggested Dimensions

Overall blank thickness: $1\frac{1}{4}$"

Shaft: $1\frac{1}{4}$" x $1\frac{1}{16}$" at throat to $1\frac{1}{16}$" x $1\frac{1}{16}$" at neck

Blade edges: $\frac{3}{32}$"

Blade thickness: $\frac{3}{8}$"

Voyageur
Blade length: 29"
Blade width: $5\frac{3}{4}$"
Surface area: 141 sq.in.

This straight-sided design has traditionally been referred to as the voyageur, even though its origin is obscure and it is certainly very different from the designs depicted by Frances Anne Hopkins in her paintings. Because of the straight line sections, the blade is relatively easy to mark out. The tip is slim and therefore enters the water quite silently, but it requires care in shallow water. An interesting feature of this paddle is that the angular recurve at the shoulder causes water to run off the edges of the blade when the paddle is moved forwards horizontally between strokes. This in-built "drip ring" stops water from running down the shaft and into the canoe. Another good paddle for deep-water touring.

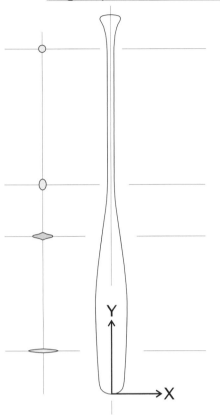

Offsets
Inches/32nds

Y	X
0/16	1/16
1	1/28
2	2/2
4	2/6
6	2/10
8	2/13
10	2/15
12	2/17
14	2/17
16	2/15
18	2/9
20	2/2
22	1/26
24	1/17
26	1/8
28	0/31
30	0/22
32	0/17

Suggested Dimensions

Overall blank thickness: $1\frac{1}{4}$"

Shaft: $1\frac{1}{4}$" x $1\frac{1}{16}$" at throat to $1\frac{1}{16}$" x $1\frac{1}{16}$" at neck

Blade edges: $\frac{3}{32}$"

Blade thickness: $\frac{3}{8}$"

Pattern for the maple leaf design

Algonquin
Blade length: 30"
Blade width: $5\frac{1}{8}$"
Surface area: 123 sq.in.

This paddle design was taken from a photograph of an authentic Algonquin paddle. The outline was captured and manipulated on computer to allow a paper pattern to be printed out. The original had a bobble grip, which I took the liberty of replacing with a contemporary pear grip. The slim blade of this paddle makes it a beauty for long-distance touring with a fairly rapid stroke rate. The tip is quite narrow, so it has a quiet entry, but it should be kept away from rocks. Submerged recovery strokes such as the Canadian stroke are easier to perform with a long, narrow blade of this type than with a lower-aspect-ratio design.

Sugar Island

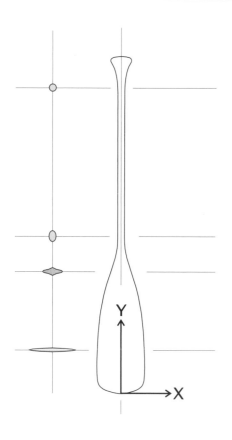

Offsets Inches/32nds	
Y	X
0/16	2/14
1	3/10
2	3/28
3	4/0
4	4/1
5	4/1
6	4/0
8	3/30
10	3/26
12	3/21
14	3/12
16	2/31
18	2/14
20	1/25
22	1/3
24	0/21
25	0/19

Suggested Dimensions

Overall blank thickness: 1¼"

Shaft: 1¼" x 1 1/16" at throat to 1 1/16" x 1 1/16" at neck

Blade edges: 3/32"

Blade thickness: 3/8"

Sugar Island
Blade length: 24"
Blade width: 8"
Surface area: 143 sq.in.

This wide paddle in designed for general river canoeing, including easy whitewater. Having most of the useful area way down the blade, it is good for steering and bracing. The paddle takes its name from the island in the St. Lawrence owned by the American Canoe Association where international canoe races between European and North American paddlers were once held. The broad tip gives good resistance to damage but a somewhat noisy entry.

Whitewater paddle

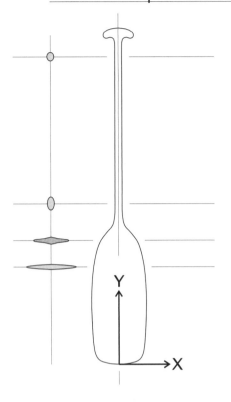

Offsets
Inches/32nds

Y	X
0/16	3/5
1	3/24
2	4/2
4	4/7
6	4/8
8	4/8
10	4/6
12	3/31
14	3/19
16	2/31
17	2/10
18	1/12
19	0/24
20	0/19

Suggested Dimensions

<u>Overall blank thickness:</u> 1 3/8"

<u>Shaft:</u> 1 3/8" x 1 1/8" at throat to 1 1/8" x 1 1/8" at neck

<u>Blade edges:</u> 3/32"

<u>Blade thickness:</u> 7/16"

Whitewater paddle
Blade length: 18 1/2"
Blade width: 8 1/2"
Surface area: 140 sq.in.

This is a low-aspect-ratio paddle designed for maneuvering in moving water. The wide blade is good for getting a grip on aerated water but would be noisy and tiring for touring. Because it is short, the blade can be kept fully submerged in shallow water. The blade area is concentrated way down the shaft for efficient steering and bracing. The construction described here is suitable only for light whitewater. For more serious conditions, you will have to consider strengthening the shaft and blade with 4-ounce fiberglass or carbon fiber cloth and epoxy resin. Fiberglass-reinforced paddles can be made out of soft,

light woods such as cedar or even balsa, which give an appreciable saving in weight. The blade template can be used to mark out suitable cloth reinforcements. This paddle has a thicker than average shaft for added strength.

Safety is a vital concern in serious whitewater. A paddle breakage could have fatal consequences. Do not venture into heavy whitewater with your home-built paddle until you have acquired sufficient experience to be certain that it will considerably exceed the structural demands made upon it. It is essential that whitewater paddles are kept properly sealed, as ingress of

water can seriously weaken them.

This design has tight curves on the grip and at the throat of the blade that are quite hard to cut out on a bandsaw; the best approach is kerf cutting, as described on page 81. The French curve sanding block helps with sanding the throat curves, and because it is quite difficult to sand the steps left by kerf cutting here, I made the prototype with strips of cherry — an easily sanded wood — in this area.

The T-grip is more easily damaged than a pear type is. For strength, the grain lines must run from side to side (when viewed from the top), rather than from front to back, and I recommend using a tough wood such as ash. The very sharp curves of the grip are not overly accessible for sand-

ing, but the job is made easier by "shoe-shining" with a very narrow strip of 60-grit paper. A good trick for sanding the tight internal strips of the grip is pull-sanding. Press an 8-by-1-inch strip of 60-grit paper into the curve with your thumb, and pull the strip through with the other hand. The thumb concentrated the pressure just where it is needed.

The tip on this paddle has a recessed ash spline in-filled with an epoxy/silica filler. Increased protection can be achieved by using several layers on glass/epoxy at the tip.

Above left: Examples of the voyageur, ottertail and whitewater. Above right: Examples of the child's beavertail, Sugar Island and Sugar Islet bent shaft.

Sugar Islet—bent-shaft paddle

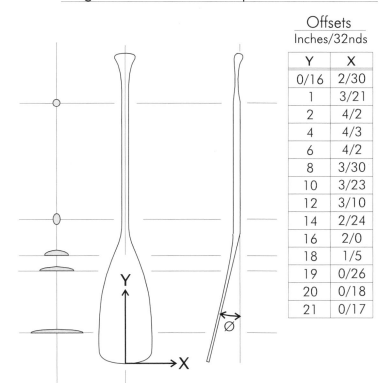

Offsets
Inches/32nds

Y	X
0/16	2/30
1	3/21
2	4/2
4	4/3
6	4/2
8	3/30
10	3/23
12	3/10
14	2/24
16	2/0
18	1/5
19	0/26
20	0/18
21	0/17

Suggested Dimensions

Shaft: 1¼" x 1¹⁄₁₆" at throat to 1¹⁄₁₆" x 1¹⁄₁₆" at neck

Blade edges: ³⁄₃₂"

Blade thickness: ³⁄₈"

Bend angle (∅): 14°

Sine 14° = 0.2419
= 7.75/32

Sugar Islet—bent shaft
Blade length: 20"
Blade width: 8¼"
Surface area: 124 sq.in.

This blade is basically a cut-down Sugar Island. The smaller blade area is designed to make the paddle less tiring for long-distance racing. Don't be tempted to add a few square inches to get an edge on your rivals; you will probably end up exhausted and fall behind. Practicing with an oversize paddle may be a useful form of "weight" training, however. The paddle shown in the illustrations has a bend of 14 degrees.

Double-blade paddle

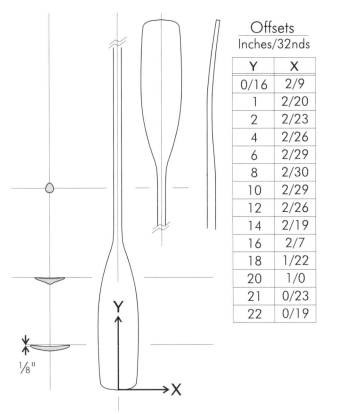

Offsets
Inches/32nds

Y	X
0/16	2/9
1	2/20
2	2/23
4	2/26
6	2/29
8	2/30
10	2/29
12	2/26
14	2/19
16	2/7
18	1/22
20	1/0
21	0/23
22	0/19

1/8"

Suggested Dimensions (softwood)

Overall blank thickness: $1\frac{1}{2}$"

Shaft: $1\frac{1}{2}$" x $1\frac{1}{4}$"

Blade edges: $\frac{3}{16}$"

Oval shaft

Power face

Initial blade thickness: $\frac{1}{2}$" (before making concave)

Power — Left control

Power — Right control

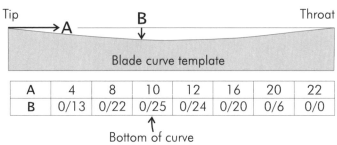

Tip →A   B↓   Throat

Blade curve template

A	4	8	10	12	16	20	22
B	0/13	0/22	0/25	0/24	0/20	0/6	0/0

Bottom of curve

Double blade

Blade length: 21"
Blade width: 6"
Surface area: 2 x 106 sq.in.

This paddle has a relatively modest blade area, which makes it suitable for reasonably long trips. Make sure that the plywood you use to make the blade template is sufficiently flexible to conform to the curve of the blade.

Child's beavertail

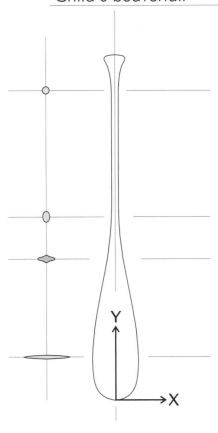

Offsets
Inches/32nds

Y	X
0/16	1/21
1	2/8
2	2/28
4	3/9
6	3/12
8	3/9
10	3/4
12	2/26
14	2/15
16	2/2
18	1/21
20	1/8
22	0/30
24	0/23
26	0/19

Suggested Dimensions

Overall blank thickness: 1⅛"

Shaft: 1⅛" x 1" at throat to 1" x 1" at neck

Blade edges: ⅛"

Blade thickness: ⁵⁄₁₆"

Child's beavertail

Blade length: 26"
Blade width: 6¾"
Surface area: 112 sq.in.

There are number of considerations when making a paddle for a child. I think that kids deserve a nice paddle and should not be sent off with a plastic thing that they don't take pride in. If they have a quality paddle, just like Mom's and Dad's, they are that much more likely to take to the canoeing experience. If it is a paddle that they have helped to make or decorate, then so much the better.

Paddles for children

There are a number of things that you should do to customize a paddle for the young canoeist. In addition to having an appropriate length, a good paddle for a child should be light and robust and have appreciable flexibility. It will have a smaller blade area than that of an adult's paddle.

• **Length**. One is always conscious that a child is continually developing and may rapidly outgrow a paddle made to fit them exactly. Children seem very adaptable in terms of use of paddles, so there should not be a problem in making their paddles a couple of inches longer than suggested by one of the sizing formulas given in Chapter 2. The paddle will fit them for that much longer.

• **Weight**. Child paddlers, especially, will appreciate a light paddle. Excess weight will simply tire them out and discourage them. I have found that in a canoeing party, a small, tired child who would rather be somewhere else is not always an asset on a trip. For a laminated paddle, my advice is to build in a lot of basswood. The shaft can be thinner than that recommended for an adult's paddle—say, 1 inch by 1 inch in hardwood—to save weight. One-piece paddles should have thin blades (e.g., $^5/_{16}$ inch) for lightness.

• **Grip**. Make sure that the grip is suitable for small hands.

• **Flexibility**. I like to build a little more flexibility into my paddles for children than I do for an adult to provide a good cushion for their joints.

• **Edges**. The blade of a child's paddle is likely to get knocked around more. It pays to leave the edges a little thicker (say a $^1/_8$ inch

instead of $^3/_{32}$ inch for a hardwood blade) to increase the resistance to chipping.

• **Decoration**. Children usually like some degree of personalization on their paddle—either a design or their initials.

It has been said that bent-shaft paddles, which are more efficient and therefore less tiring over a given distance, are especially suitable for children.

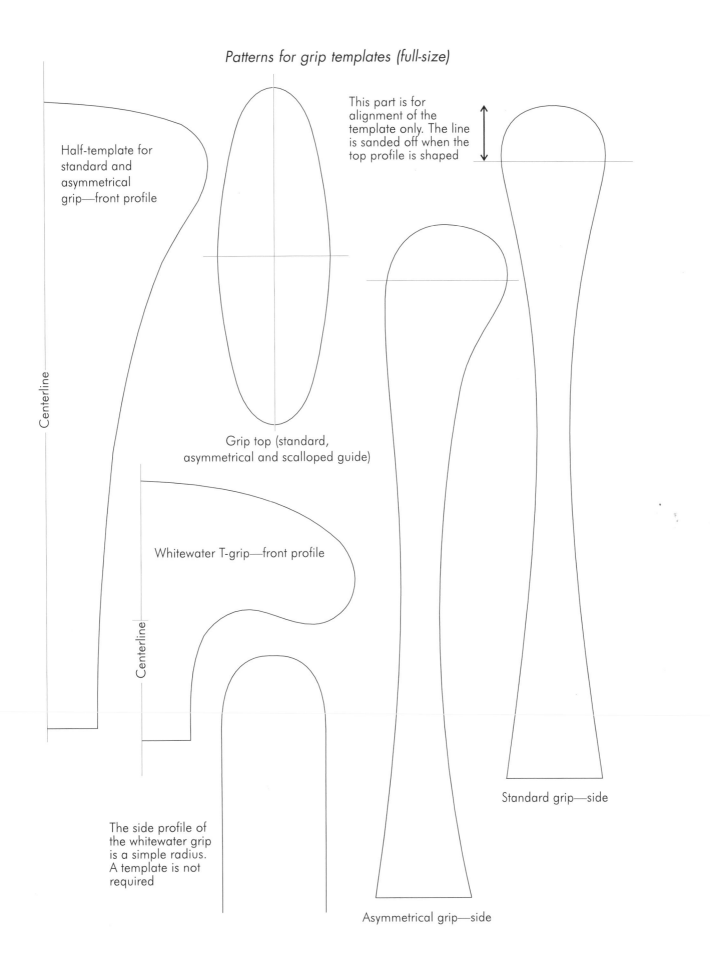

Patterns for grip templates (full-size)

Half-template for standard and asymmetrical grip—front profile

This part is for alignment of the template only. The line is sanded off when the top profile is shaped

Centerline

Grip top (standard, asymmetrical and scalloped guide)

Whitewater T-grip—front profile

Centerline

The side profile of the whitewater grip is a simple radius. A template is not required

Asymmetrical grip—side

Standard grip—side

Scalloped guide grip

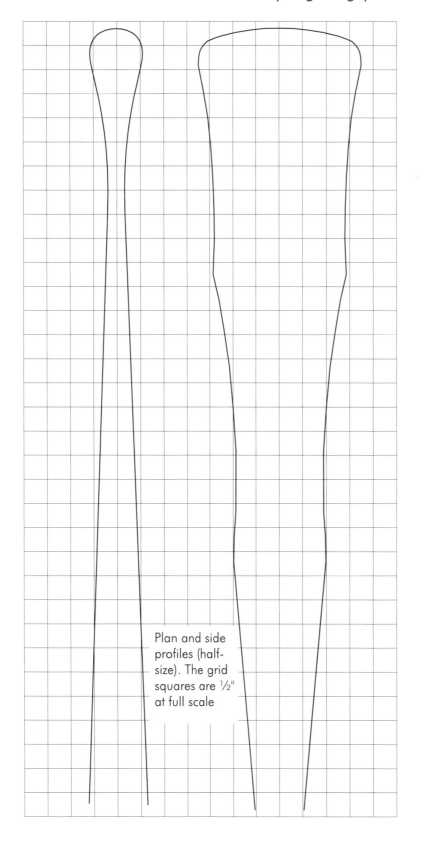

Plan and side
profiles (half-
size). The grid
squares are ½"
at full scale

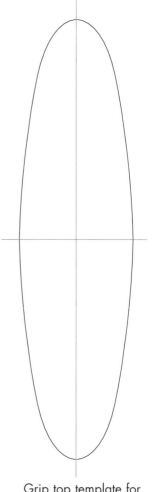

Grip top template for
whitewater T-grip (full-size)

Grip plans

From an almost limitless number
of designs for paddle grips, I have
selected four that give a reasonable amount of variety. Although
the dimensions were chosen to fit
my hands, many people have tried
these grips and generally found
them comfortable. You may want
to modify the dimensions to suit
your own personal requirements.

Tip and throat templates (full-size)

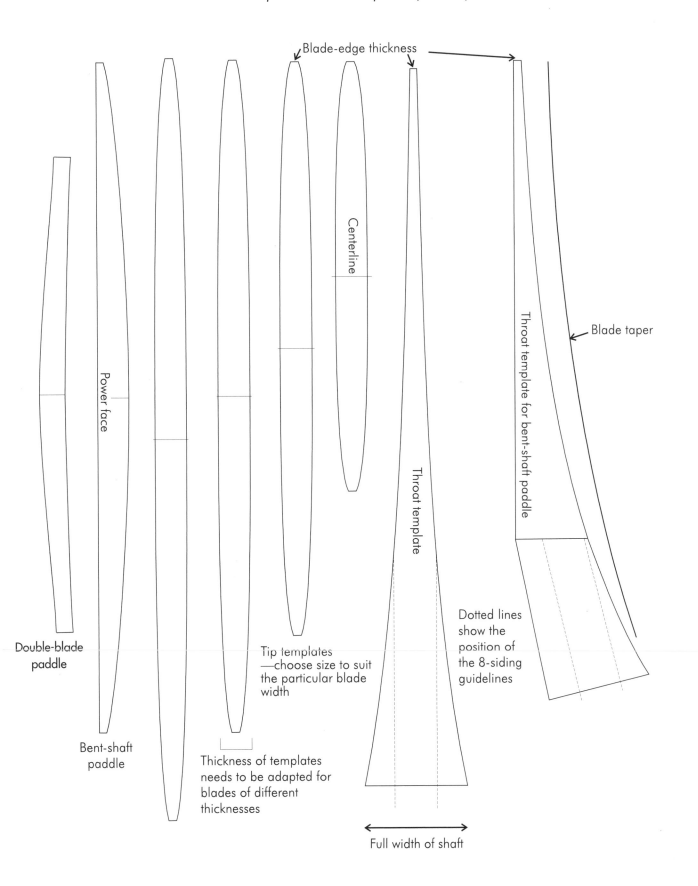

Blade-edge thickness

Centerline

Power face

Throat template for bent-shaft paddle

Throat template

Blade taper

Double-blade paddle

Bent-shaft paddle

Tip templates —choose size to suit the particular blade width

Thickness of templates needs to be adapted for blades of different thicknesses

Full width of shaft

Dotted lines show the position of the 8-siding guidelines

Glossary

Angled grain. Any intermediate grain configuration between edge grain and flat grain.

Aspect ratio. The length of a paddle blade divided by its width. A blade with a high aspect ratio is long and thin; a paddle with a low aspect ratio is short and wide.

Blade face. The newly exposed face of a strip of wood as it comes off a saw.

Blade wings. The outer strips that form the blade edges in laminated paddles.

Blank. Wood cut to a basic paddle shape.

Bookmatched. Mirror-image grain configuration on either side of center in the blade or grip of a laminated paddle.

Breakout. When the parallel grain lines are at an angle to the long axis of a piece of wood.

Camber. The gentle convex curve of the surface of a paddle blade.

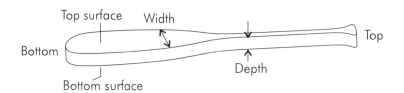

Terminology

Top surface   Width   Top
Bottom
Bottom surface   Depth

Contained grain. Refers to strips of wood in which the grain lines are parallel to the long dimension of the strip.

Dihedral. The angled surface on some paddle blades that gives a diamond cross section.

Drag. A blanket term for the resistance shown by a paddle blade to water flowing around it.

Edge-grain paddle. A paddle made from wood in which the growth rings are perpendicular to the blade surface.

Edge marking. Marking a carving guideline with transverse pencil hatches to give a better visual indicator of the removal of wood.

End grain. The exposed surface when wood is cut directly across the growth rings, such as when a tree is felled.

External curve. A convex surface.

Fair. When the shape of the wood conforms exactly to the pattern. Also refers to lines that are absolutely straight or curves that are smooth and flowing.

Flat-grain paddle. A paddle made from wood in which the growth rings run more or less parallel to the blade surface.

Flats. The flat tracks left by strokes of a plane, spokeshave or similar tool.

Hydrocycling. The swelling and shrinking of wood resulting from increases and decreases in the water content.

Internal curve. A concave surface.

Laminating beam. A perfectly flat piece of wood to which strips are clamped when making the shaft of a laminated paddle.

Neck. The region of a paddle where the grip merges into the shaft.

Outline shape. The shape of a paddle laid on a flat surface and viewed from directly overhead.

Quarters. The four half-faces of a paddle blade. Because most blades are symmetrical, shaping operations carried out in one region of the blade have to be repeated in the three other equivalent areas.

Quarter-sawn wood. Boards resulting from a log being cut first into quarters, then slices being taken from flat sides of each quarter. The growth rings are perpendicular to the faces of the boards.

Overwidth/overdepth. Refers to a strip of wood that is cut larger (usually by around $1/8$ inch) than the required dimension to allow for planing.

Reference. The edge or face of the wood that is used as a baseline for marking out from or to guide the wood along the fence of a power saw or bed of a planer.

Shoulders. The edges of a paddle blade just below the throat.

Softening. Paddling placed between a clamp and the wood it is holding to prevent bruising.

Spine. The ridge running from the shaft partway down the center of the blade.

Spline. A thin strip of wood set crossways into the tip of a blade to help resist splitting.

Spooned blade. A blade that is curved both from top to bottom and from side to side, like a spoon.

Table face. The face of a strip of wood being cut on a bandsaw that is in contact with the saw table.

Throat. The region of a paddle where the blade merges into the shaft.

True. Usually refers to a piece of wood that is straight and square-edged.

Resources

I am maintaining a website at http://homepages.tesco.net/~moosehead/ as a place to exchange information on the techniques and designs contained in this book, as well as ideas on all aspects of paddlemaking. I will be pleased to receive details of new or modified paddlemaking techniques and of the location of native paddles in museums and collections via email at Moosehead@tesco.net

Templates set for the paddles described here (including those for carving guidelines) can be obtained from Moosehead Canoes, 23, Broomhill Road, Old Whittington, Chesterfield, Derbyshire S41 9DB, U.K. Computer files to allow you to print out a paper blade pattern from any of the plans or paddles in the line illustrations in this book are also available.

Museum collections
The following is a small selection of the many museums that have collections of native paddles:
North America
The Adirondack Museum, Blue Mountain Lake, NY;
The American Museum of Natural History, New York, NY;

The Canadian Canoe Museum, Peterborough, ON;
Madeline Island Historical Museum, La Pointe, WI;
The Mariners' Museum, Newport News, VA;
McCord Museum of Canadian History, Montreal, QC;
The National Museum of the American Indian, Heye Center, New York, NY;
The Peabody Museum of Archaeology and Ethnology, Harvard University, Cambridge, MA

United Kingdom
Arbuthnot Museum, Peterhead, Scotland (a small but important collection of Inuit artifacts);
The British Museum, London;
The National Maritime Museum, Greenwich, London

Paddlemaking websites
A good place to start on the web is the site of the Wooden Canoe Heritage Association, http://www.wcha.org. This site features a series of articles on making various types of paddles (http://www.wcha.org/tidbits/index.html), as well as a bulletin board where you can ask for information related to paddlemaking

from the site's very knowledgeable user base. The association's on-line Builders and Suppliers Directory lists paddlemakers by country and state.

The newsgroups rec.boats.paddle, rec.boats.building and rec.woodworking are also excellent sources of information.

A search of the web will bring up many pages by commercial paddlemakers who often have information of paddle design and materials, as well as pictures of paddles, which are a source of ideas.

Paddlemaking classes
Keith Backlund, Backlund Paddles
26115 Clarksburg Road
Clarksburg, MD 20871
Email: backlundpaddles@juno.com
Keith runs one-day repair clinics and two- and five-day courses on making top-quality laminated paddles sheathed in fiberglass.

Caleb Davis (NH)
Email: tremolo@together.net.
www.wcha.org/builders/tremolo
Classes on making one-piece paddles.

David Gidmark
Box 26, Maniwaki, QC J9E 3B3
(819) 438-2382
Classes on making paddles in the traditional way, with ax and crooked knife. David also runs courses on making birchbark canoes.

Philip Greene
Wood Song Canoes
425 Jessie Lane
Round O
SC 29474
pgreene@lowcountry.com
Philip Greene gives a detailed lecture on making fine laminated paddles.

Douglas Ingram
Red River Canoe & Paddle
19 River Road
P.O. Box 78, Grp 4, RR 2
Lorette, MB ROA OYO
(204) 878-2524
Email: redcanoe@pangea.ca
www.wilds.mb.ca/redriver
Courses by arrangement.

Graham Warren
Moosehead Canoes
23, Broomhill Road,
Old Whittington, Chesterfield,
Derbyshire S41 9DB, U.K.

Classes on one-piece and laminated paddles.

Suppliers
Plans and templates

Moosehead Canoes
23 Broomhill Road
Old Whittington, Chesterfield,
Derbyshire, S41 9DB, UK
Email: Moosehead@tesco.net
http://www.wcha.org/builders/moosehead
http://homepages.tesco.net/~moosehead/
Templates set (including those for carving guidelines) for the paddles described in this book and 30 other paddle designs.

Keith Backlund
Backlund Paddles
26115 Clarksburg Road
Clarksburg, MD 20871
Email: backlundpaddles@juno.com
Blade patterns and templates for his highly rated range of single and double paddles.

Douglas Ingram
Red River Canoe & Paddle:
address as above
Patterns for a range of native and contemporary styles.

Paddle blanks

Graham Warren, Moosehead Canoes: address as above.

Douglas Ingram, Red River Canoe & Paddle: address as above.

Woods

North America
Local sawmills are the best source of wood, but you may be limited to the species harvested in your area.

An excellent on-line resource is Woodweb (http://www.woodweb.com). This contains a lumber-buying guide that provides sources across North America and also presents a marketplace for used woodworking machinery.

Keith Backlund sells high-quality northern white ash and black willow. Keith takes extraordinary care in selecting the wood especially for paddlemaking. Other species available. Contact Backlund Paddles, address as above.

Philip Greene, Wood Song Canoes: address as above

United Kingdom
John Boddy
Riverside Sawmills
Boroughbridge, N. Yorks, YO5 9LJ

Fitchett and Woolacott Ltd.
Willow Road, Lenton Lane
Nottingham, NG7 2PR

Adhesives

North America
Adhesives should be available
locally, but in case of difficulty,
major distributors or the manufacturers can be contacted.

West Epoxy

Gougeon Brothers, Inc.
100 Patterson Avenue
P.O. Box 908
Bay City, MI 48707-0908
Phone (517) 684-7286
http://www.gougeon.com

Polyurethane Glue (Excel, Titebond, Gorilla)

The Ambel Corporation
(800) 779-3935 or (318) 876-2495
http://www.excelglue.com
Email: excelglue@aol.com

Franklin International
2020 Bruck Street
Columbus, OH 43207
(800) 877-4583
(614) 443-0241
http://www.covinax.com/tite
bond.htm

Lutz File and Tool Company,
3929 Virginia Avenue
Cincinnati, OH 45227
Phone: (513) 271-3300
Fax: (513) 527-3742
Email: lutz@iglou.com
http://www.gorillaglue.com
Has a search engine for local
suppliers.

Urea-formaldehyde (Cascamite, Aerolite) and resorcinol (Cascophen, Penacolite)

Allred & Associates, Inc.
5566 Jordan Road
Elbridge, NY 13060
Phone: (315) 689-1626
Fax: (315) 689-1438
Email: carvers@dreamscape.com
http://www.wood
carver.com/store.html

Wicks Aircraft Supply
Phone: (800) 221-9425
Email: info@wicks.com
http://www.wicksaircraft.com/

United Kingdom
Robbins Timber
Merrywood Road
Bedminster, Bristol, BS3 1DX

Oil and Varnish

Epifanes varnish

Epifanes North America, Inc.
58 Fore Street
Portland, ME 04101
Phone: (207) 775-1333
Fax: (207) 775-1551
http://www.epifanes.com
Email: epifanes@maine.com

International Varnish

http://www.yachtpaint.com/usa/
1-800-Intrlux (1-800-468-7589)

Cetol

Specialty Products Center
Finishes' Supply
545 Turner Drive
Durango, CO 81301
(970) 259-8445
(888) 840-8445
Email: info@logfinishers.com
http://www.sikkens.com/talen.html

Deks Olje/Watco

Jamestown Distributors
28 Narragansett Avenue
P.O. Box 348
Jamestown, RI 02835
Phone: (800) 423-0030
or (401) 423-2520
Fax: (800) 423-0542
or (401) 423-0542
Email: info@jamestowndistribu

tors.com http://jamestowndistrib
utors.com/products/finishwork.htm

Boiled linseed oil is available at
just about any hardware store.
Tung oil should be available at
the larger stores.

Breakdown joints for double-blade paddles

Chesapeake Light Craft, Inc.
1805 George Avenue
Annapolis, MD 21401
Phone: (410) 267-0137
Fax: (301) 858-6335
Email: kayaks@clcinc.com
http://www.clcboats.com/

Crooked knives

David Fleming
Box 192
Cobden, ON K0J 1K0
Phone: (613) 646-2356
Crooked knives made on order,
US$45 and up.

Howard Guptill
Box 285
Happy Valley, NF A0P 1E0
Phone: (709) 896-8055
Crooked knives made on order;
US$75 and up.

Paddle bags

Alder Stream Canvas
Jane Barron
RR 1, Box 1550
Kingfield, ME 04947

Miscellaneous

Powdered silica (300 mesh) for
blade tips
Moosehead Canoes (UK): address
as above.

Further Reading

Books

Adney, Edwin Tappan and Chapelle, Howard I. *The Bark Canoes and Skin Boats of North America.* Smithsonian Institution Press, Washington, 1983. The classic reference book.

Black, Martha. *Bella Bella: A Season of Heiltsuk Art.* University of Washington Press, 1997. Contains illustrations of Northwest Coast paddles.

Edwards, Robert. *Aboriginal Bark Canoes of the Murray Valley.* Adelaide, 1972.

Frid, Tage. *Tage Frid Teaches Woodworking.* The Taunton Press, Connecticut, 1993. Excellent information on all aspects of woodworking.

Gidmark, David. *Birchbark Canoe: Living Among the Algonquin.* Firefly Books, Toronto, 1997. Learning birchbark canoe building with the last of the Algonquin master builders.

_____. *Building a Birchbark Canoe: The Algonquin Wâbanäki Tcîmân.* Firefly Books, Toronto, 2001. Methods of construction of the birchbark canoe by four Algonquin builders. Extensive glossary (in Algonquin) and useful bibliography.

_____. *The Indian Crafts of William and Mary Commanda.* Firefly Books, Toronto, 2001. The Commandas make birchbark canoes, snowshoes, cradle boards and do such crafts as hide-tanning and quillwork.

Jenkins, J. Geraint. *The Coracle.* Golden Grove, Wales, 1988.

Kent, Tim. *Birchbark Canoes of the Fur Trade.* Information on voyageur paddles. Currently out of print.

McCarthy, Henry "Mac". *Featherweight Boatbuilding.* WoodenBoat, 1996. Gives instructions for making double-blade paddles.

Martensson, Alf. *The Woodworker's Bible.* A&C Black, London, 1984. In-depth information about hand and power tools and the properties of woods.

Stelmok, Jerry and Thurlow, Rollin. *The Wood and Canvas Canoe.* The Harpswell Press, Maine, 1987. Details on how to make a drum sander.

Taylor, J. Garth. *Canoe Construction in a Cree Cultural Tradition.* National Museums of Canada, Ottawa, 1980. An excellent book that shows traditional canoe construction and paddlemaking by master Cree craftsman John Kawapit.

Various Authors. *Wood and How to Dry It.* Fine Woodworking. The Taunton Press, Connecticut, 1986. A detailed resource on seasoning wood and the responses of wood to moisture.

Warren, Graham. *Making Canoe Paddles in Wood.* Raven Rock Books, England, 1977. Available from Moosehead Canoes, UK. Contains additional hints for making paddles, including ideas for laminating, details of spar gauges, a leather throat protector and a copper blade tip; model paddles, computer-aided design and how to carve features seen on native paddles. Has 10 additional paddle designs, with history of each.

_____. *Advanced Paddlemaking.* In preparation. Raven Rock Books, England. Information on using difficult woods, data on wood and adhesive testing, balancing a paddle, more tools and jigs, computer-aided design and software, plastic blade tips and using glass and carbon fiber for ultralight paddles. Contains 50 paddle designs; contemporary, native and experimental.

Winters, John. *The Shape of the Canoe.* Available from Redwing Designs, RR 2, 319 Berriedale Road, Burk's Falls, Ontario P0A 1C0. Email: 735769@ican.net

Wright, Robin, K. *A Time of Gathering.* University of Washington Press, 1992. Information on Northwest Coast paddles.

Zimmerly, David. W. *Qayaq: Kayaks of Alaska and Siberia.* University of Alaska Press, Fairbanks, 2000. A remarkably valuable book on the construction of a variety of Inuit kayaks and the paddles used with them. Fascinating historical photos.

Articles

Andersen, Søren H. "Mesolithic dugouts and paddles from Tybrind Vig, Denmark." *Acta Archaeologica* vol. 57, 87-106, 1986.

Broze, Matt. "A quest for the perfect paddle." *Sea Kayaker,* Spring 1992.

Davis, Caleb. "A good paddle." *Wooden Canoe* #87, 1998.

Davis, Jack. "Wooden paddle repair and restoration." *Wooden Canoe* #82, 1997.

Spielbauer, Arnie. "Carving a traditional wooden paddle." *Wooden Canoe* #57, 1993.

Back issues of *Wooden Canoe* are available from The Wooden Canoe Heritage Association, P.O. Box 226. Blue Mountain Lake, New York 12812.

Back issues of *WoodenBoat* contain several articles of single- and double-blade paddles. An index is available from the publishers.

Also by David Gidmark

"Birchbark Canoe is the story of how I learned birchbark canoe building from three of the last master Algonquin birchbark builders. Framed by the birchbark canoe itself, this story gives a look at the generosity, warmth and good humor of the Algonquin people." — **DG**

BIRCHBARK CANOE
LIVING AMONG THE ALGONQUIN

• *"Includes a first-rate series of color photographs showing the construction of a canoe…a fascinating book."*

—**WoodenBoat magazine**, *Brooklin, Maine*

• *"The pleasures of this book are such that…I read it through without stopping."*

—**The Beaver**, *Winnipeg, Manitoba*

• *"A Canadian outdoor classic."*

—**CBC News**

• *"Although he never met Tappan Adney, David Gidmark may be his most successful student."*

—**Telegraph Journal**, *Saint John, New Brunswick*

Discover the disappearing art of birchbark canoe building through the eyes of someone who is passionate about it. In this book, Gidmark tells the story of building a traditional birchbark canoe and of his apprenticeship learning the skills and the language of the Algonquin of western Quebec.

Through learning how to strip the bark from the tree, fashion gunwales from the cedar logs, carve the ribs with a crooked knife and sew the huge sheets of bark onto the frame with spruce root, Gidmark also learns how to relate to the wilderness in Algonquin ways that are very different from ours. As his knowledge increases, so does his respect for the culture and wisdom of native peoples.

For over 10 years, David Gidmark has lived deep in the woods of Quebec. He teaches canoe building in Wisconsin, New York, Tahiti and Quebec.

Birchbark Canoe is published by

FIREFLY BOOKS

and available through bookstores everywhere.
ISBN 1-55209-150-3